marie claire

spicy

Thunder Bay Press
An imprint of the Advantage Publishers Group
5880 Oberlin Drive, San Diego, CA 92121-4794
www.thunderbaybooks.com

All notations of errors or omissions should be addressed to Thunder Bay Press, Editorial Department, at the above address. All other correspondence (author inquiries, permissions) concerning the content of this book should be addressed to Murdoch Books Pty Limited, Pier 8/9 23 Hickson Road, Millers Point NSW 2000 Australia.

Author and Stylist: Michele Cranston   Photographer: Petrina Tinslay
Design manager: Vivien Valk   Concept: Lauren Camilleri
Food preparation: Ross Dobson and Jo Glynn   Designer: Jacqueline Richards
Production: Monika Paratore   Editor: Gordana Trifunovic

ISBN-13: 978-1-59223-662-6
ISBN-10: 1-59223-662-6
Library of Congress Cataloging-in-Publication Data available upon request.

Printed by 1010 Printing. Printed in China.
1 2 3 4 5 10 09 08 07 06

IMPORTANT: Those who might be at risk from the effects of salmonella poisoning (the elderly, pregnant women, young children, and those suffering from immune deficiency diseases) should consult their doctor with any concerns about eating raw eggs.

CONVERSION GUIDE: You may find cooking times vary depending on the oven you are using. For convection ovens, as a general rule, set the oven temperature to 70°F lower than indicated in the recipe. We have used 4 teaspoon to 1 tablespoon measurements. If you are using a 3 teaspoon to 1 tablespoon measure, for most recipes the difference will not be noticeable. However, for recipes using baking powder, gelatin, baking soda, or small amounts of flour and cornstarch, add an extra teaspoon for each tablespoon specified.

marie claire
spicy

michele cranston
photography by petrina tinslay

THUNDER BAY
P · R · E · S · S
San Diego, California

contents

Welcome to *Marie Claire Spicy,* a selection of our favorite recipes that are warm and inviting, richly flavored, sweetly spiced, or just simple food with a bit of a twist. We hope this thick and hearty book will inspire you with lots of yummy ideas for everything from easy dips and spiced nuts to peppered beef, richly flavored curries, and exotic desserts.

I've had a lot of fun revisiting old favorites, and I hope that you have as much fun cooking and eating from our selection.

michele cranston

ingredient note

figs

A perfect fig is a wonderful thing to behold and to sink your teeth into. I first fell in love with figs when backpacking through Greece. Up and around early in the morning I stumbled upon a market square. One of the stalls had big vats of creamy yogurt. The yogurt was served in a cup with a swirl of wild honey, and the stall next door sold fresh figs, straight from the tree and warmed by the early morning sun. I don't think I've ever had a better breakfast!

However, figs are one of those rare fruits that do have a distinct season, and they are only available on the market shelves for a short time. So when they do finally appear, don't just limit their use to the odd sumptuous breakfast—they can and should be enjoyed at any time of the day. Served with goat cheese, arugula leaves, and a sweet balsamic dressing, they become an indulgent lunch. Wrapped with prosciutto they make a wonderful start to an evening meal, and with a pile of muscatels they make the perfect accompaniment to a selection of soft cheeses.

Spices, nuts, and cream also complement figs, so there is no excuse not to use them for a tempting selection of desserts. They can be baked into a tart of sugary sweetness or freshly sliced over small tartlets filled with sweet mascarpone cheese. Bake them whole with the addition of soft brown sugar and Marsala, arrange fresh slices over meringue, or, simply cut in half, sprinkle with sugar, and broil. That's the great thing about figs—already so perfect, they need very little work to turn them into a celebratory ending to any meal.

ingredient note   # rhubarb

I have to admit to a love of rhubarb that goes back to my childhood. My grandfather had a wonderful vegetable garden, and one section was devoted to rhubarb. As a young child I would gaze at the exuberant red stalks that stood out from the green mass of fresh herbs, spinach leaves, and carrot tops. Naturally, my grandfather always seemed to have a bowl of stewed rhubarb in the refrigerator, which would be spooned over ice cream, custard, and even the odd bowl of breakfast cereal.

Rhubarb is actually a vegetable, and although it can be used in stews with meat, it really comes into its own when cooked with just enough sugar to cut its sharpness. Always look for stalks that are a rich red and that show no signs of softening. Trim the leaves and cut the rhubarb into small pieces before cooking over low heat with some sugar or with the addition of orange juice, vanilla, star anise, or fresh ginger.

Rhubarb is available all year-round, making it an ideal addition to the dessert repertoire in those cooler months when the fruit selection can seem a little dismal. It's wonderful when added to apple and pear for a winter crumble, stewed and spooned over mini pavlovas, or served alongside crème brûlées to cut their richness. For a lighter touch, simply bake and serve with creamy custard and amaretti cookies, or fold a puree of rhubarb through whipped cream for a simple tangy dessert.

eggplant

There really is something quite beautiful about eggplants. I always think they look as if they've been sculpted into shape and then heavily burnished to that wonderful purple-black color. I have to admit that I do often buy them merely as beautiful objects to put in my kitchen. Fortunately I also love to eat them, so there's no waste!

Eggplants grilled over a barbecue or gas flame take on a wonderful smoky flavor that makes for a perfect dip when mixed with a bit of lemon juice, tahini, and a light sprinkling of parsley leaves. Barbecued slices can be tossed with parsley, cilantro, or basil and added to tomato and pine nuts for a simple vegetable side dish. Fried in small bite-sized chunks, it becomes a meaty addition to vegetable stews and curries or a hearty accompaniment to that famous eggplant dish, moussaka. Thinly sliced and deep fried, eggplant makes a great addition to any salad, or it can be used crisp for dipping. Although usually associated with European and Middle Eastern cooking, the eggplant also works well with the Asian flavors of soy, ginger, and chili, as well as being an important ingredient in many Thai curries.

There seems to be some debate as to whether eggplants need to be salted. This time-consuming process shouldn't be necessary with small or very fresh eggplants. The salting is merely to draw out any bitterness, which can sometimes occur in older or larger eggplants. However, salting does help if you need to fry the eggplant, since the process prevents the pieces from soaking up too much oil.

ingredient note   # saffron

There's something evocative about spices. Whenever I use them I try to remember the wonderful history of ancient trade routes and people traveling long distances to discover new cuisines with exotic tastes and aromas. If ever a spice lived up to such heady notions, then saffron is the one. Each golden strand is handpicked from the purple crocus flower. It is then dried and sold as, not surprisingly, a very expensive spice. But don't let the price stop you from buying a small amount, especially if it comes from Spain, which reputedly harvests the best in the world. You only need a small amount when you're cooking, and it really does infuse any meal with a wonderful taste and a golden hue.

As a flavor, saffron is ideally suited to seafood dishes and makes an appearance in such classics as bouillabaisse and paella. Although perfectly suited to seafood, it can also be used with vegetables and fruit. Toss a little saffron-tinged water in with leeks that have been basted in lots of butter, salt, pepper, and a little chicken stock, or for a golden dessert, add a tiny amount to the poaching liquid for pears.

To get the most out of your saffron, I find it is best to first heat it over a low flame in the base of a saucepan and to then pour a little water over the top. This allows the intense flavor and yellow color to be transferred to the liquid. It is then quite easy to add it to any dish, whether it is baked, stewed, or simmered.

beet dip bread sticks tabouleh eggplant
pinwheels quail eggs with za'atar mix eggplant dip
spiced nut blend baked baby eggplant with miso
spiced potato chips spicy nut cookies eggplant
rounds with sweet harissa and mint hummus watermelon
squares welsh rarebit chili beef on belgian endive
leaves lime and cashew cod rolls gravlax with dill
dressing on pumpernickel salt and pepper tofu spiced

01 starters and sides

pan bread taramasalata sweet-potato chips with baba
ghanoush roasted vegetables with rouille spiced red
cabbage fennel salad bulgur salad roasted beet salad
papaya and coconut sambal warm banana-chili salad
puy lentil and spinach salad fattoush rice

beet dip

4 large beets
1 cup yogurt
1 teaspoon pomegranate molasses
sea salt and freshly ground black
  pepper, to season
10 mint leaves, finely chopped
10 walnuts, finely chopped
toasted pita bread, to serve

Preheat the oven to 400°F. Place the beets in a roasting pan with 1 cup of water. Cover with foil and roast for 1 hour, or until cooked. Rub the skin off the beets.

Place the beets in a food processor or blender and blend to a smooth paste. Put in a bowl and stir in the yogurt and pomegranate molasses. Season to taste with sea salt and freshly ground black pepper. Garnish with the mint and walnuts, and serve with toasted pita bread.

bread sticks

2 teaspoons dried yeast or 1/2 ounce
  fresh yeast
1/2 teaspoon sugar
2 1/2 cups all-purpose flour
2 tablespoons black sesame seeds
1 tablespoon freshly ground cumin
  seeds
2 tablespoons chopped thyme
1/2 teaspoon sea salt, plus extra for
  sprinkling
1 egg
1 tablespoon olive oil

Mix the yeast, 1 cup warm water, and the sugar in a bowl. Leave to sit for 10 minutes. Put the flour, sesame seeds, cumin, thyme, and salt in a bowl and make a well in the center. Pour in the yeast mixture and mix to form a soft dough. Gather into a ball, turn out onto a floured surface, and knead for 10 minutes. Place in an oiled bowl, cover with plastic wrap, and leave for 3 hours in a warm place.

When the dough has doubled in size, punch it down and turn out onto a floured surface. Knead for 2 minutes, then roll the dough out to a thickness of 1/4 inch. Cut into strips approximately 10 x 1/2 inches. Roll and place onto baking sheets lined with parchment paper. Cover and allow to rise for 30 minutes.

Preheat the oven to 350°F. In a bowl, beat the egg with 3 tablespoons of water. Brush the dough with the egg wash. Bake for 15 minutes or until golden. Remove from the oven, brush with olive oil, and sprinkle with sea salt. Return to the oven for an additional 4–5 minutes or until golden. Allow to cool on a wire rack.

tabouleh

heaping 1/3 cup bulgur wheat
3 ripe tomatoes, finely chopped
sea salt and freshy ground black
  pepper, to season
1 bunch (about 5 1/2 ounces) Italian
  parsley
2 scallions, finely chopped
1 small handful mint, finely chopped
4 tablespoons olive oil
3 tablespoons lemon juice

Soak the bulgur wheat in cold water for 10 minutes, then drain and squeeze to remove any excess water. Put the bulgur in a large bowl and add the tomatoes. Season with sea salt and freshly ground black pepper. Finely chop the parsley, gathering the leafy ends together and discarding the stems. Add to the salad with the onions and mint. Combine the olive oil and lemon juice and pour over the salad. Toss together and serve.

eggplant pinwheels

2 red bell peppers, trimmed and
  seeds removed
4–5 medium (about 14 ounces)
  zucchini
50 large basil leaves
1 tablespoon balsamic vinegar
3 tablespoons olive oil
1 large eggplant, thinly sliced
  lengthwise

Broil or roast the bell peppers and set aside to cool. With a vegetable peeler, slice the zucchini into long ribbons. Blanch the zucchini ribbons and basil leaves in boiling water for a few seconds and refresh in cold water. Peel the cooked bell peppers and slice the flesh in half. Toss with the vinegar.

Heat the oil in a large frying pan over medium heat and cook the eggplant slices until soft. Drain on paper towels.

Lay a piece of parchment paper or plastic wrap on the work surface and arrange a single line of overlapping eggplant slices. Cover with a layer of zucchini, then a layer of bell pepper, and finally a layer of basil. Roll up firmly to form a thin log. Repeat with the remaining ingredients. Refrigerate until ready to use. Slice and serve.

quail eggs with za'atar mix

serves 6-8

2 tablespoons sesame seeds,
   lightly toasted
1 tablespoon thyme leaves
1 tablespoon ground sumac
1/2 teaspoon ground cumin
1 teaspoon sea salt
24 quail eggs, boiled and shelled

Mix together the sesame seeds,
spices, and sea salt. Serve in a bowl
accompanied by the quail eggs.

eggplant dip

serves 6-8

2 tablespoons oil
1 garlic bulb
1 large eggplant
4 tablespoons tahini
2 tablespoons lemon juice
sea salt, to season
2 tablespoons finely chopped
  Italian parsley
cayenne pepper, for sprinkling
crusty bread, to serve

Preheat the oven to 400°F. Put the oil in a small roasting pan. Cut the garlic bulb across the middle so that the cloves are cut in half. Put each garlic half, cut side down, in the oiled pan and add the eggplant. Bake for 20 minutes or until the garlic halves are golden brown and the eggplant is soft. Remove from the oven and allow to cool.

With the tip of a small sharp knife, separate the garlic cloves from the bulb and put them in a blender or food processor. Cut the eggplant in half, scoop out the soft flesh, and add it to the garlic. Blend to a puree.

Transfer to a bowl and fold through the tahini and lemon juice. Season with sea salt. Just before serving, fold the parsley through and sprinkle with cayenne pepper. Serve with crusty bread.

spiced nut blend

makes 2¹/2 cups

1 teaspoon cumin seeds
1 teaspoon coriander seeds
1 teaspoon mustard seeds
1/4 teaspoon fennel seeds
1/2 cinnamon stick
1/2 teaspoon black peppercorns
1 teaspoon ground turmeric
2 tablespoons soft brown sugar
2 1/4 cups mixed nuts, including
   pecans, cashew nuts, peanuts,
   and macadamia nuts
2 teaspoons sea salt
2 tablespoons olive oil

Preheat the oven to 315°F. Place all the spices in a spice grinder or blender and grind to a fine powder. Transfer the mixture to a large bowl and mix in the sugar, nuts, and sea salt. Add the olive oil, mix well, and place on a baking sheet. Bake for 10–15 minutes, or until the nuts have browned a little. Allow to cool. Store in an airtight container until ready to serve.

baked baby eggplant
with miso
makes 20

1/4 cup white miso paste
1 tablespoon sugar
1 tablespoon mirin
1 egg yolk
2 teaspoons fresh ginger juice
10 baby eggplants
3/4 cup vegetable oil
1 tablespoon sesame seeds

Put the miso, sugar, and mirin in a large bowl. Add the egg yolk and lightly whisk. Place the bowl over a saucepan of boiling water, whisking continuously while slowly adding 4 tablespoons of cold water. Keep whisking until the mixture is thick. Stir the ginger juice through the mixture.

Preheat the oven to 375°F. Slice each eggplant in half lengthwise and trim the skin side so that the halves sit flat. Heat the oil in a deep frying pan over medium heat and cook the eggplants on both sides until they are golden and slightly soft. Remove and drain on paper towels.

Place the eggplants on a baking sheet and spread with a little of the miso paste. Sprinkle with the sesame seeds and bake for 5 minutes.

spiced potato chips

makes 30

1 teaspoon sesame seeds
1/2 teaspoon ground cumin
1/2 teaspoon ground coriander
1/2 teaspoon ground paprika
2 large roasting potatoes, peeled
1 1/2 tablespoons unsalted butter, melted

Preheat the oven to 325°F. Combine the sesame seeds and spices in a small bowl. Slice the potatoes very thinly and place half the slices on a baking sheet lined with parchment paper. Top each slice of potato with another slice, preferably of a similar size, and press together. (The starch in the potatoes will stick them together.) Brush with butter and sprinkle with the spice mix.

Bake for 45 minutes, or until the potatoes are crisp and golden brown. Drain on paper towels and serve.

spicy nut cookies

makes 55

1 tablespoon grated fresh ginger

1 green chili, seeded and finely chopped

1¹/₃ cups cashew nuts

²/₃ cup pistachio nuts

1¹/₄ cups rice flour

1¹/₂ teaspoons ground cumin

2 tablespoons roughly chopped cilantro leaves

1 tablespoon black sesame seeds

1¹/₂ tablespoons butter

2 eggs, beaten

²/₃ cup vegetable oil

Put the ginger, chili, cashew nuts, pistachios, rice flour, cumin, cilantro, sesame seeds, butter, and 2 teaspoons of salt in a food processor. Pulse a few times to grind the nuts, then transfer to a large bowl. Add the eggs and 3 tablespoons of water. Stir until the mixture combines and is sticky.

Take a heaping teaspoon of the mixture, roll it into a ball, and flatten it slightly. Heat the oil in a deep frying pan over low heat. Take a few of the flattened balls and place into the oil. Cook for 5 minutes, turning once, until golden brown. Drain on paper towels. Repeat with the remaining mixture.

eggplant rounds with sweet harissa and mint

makes 24

4 baby or Japanese eggplants

salt, for sprinkling

2/3 cup vegetable oil

2 red bell peppers, roasted, skins
  removed

2 teaspoons roasted ground cumin

2 teaspoons roasted ground coriander

2 small red chilies, seeded and finely
  chopped

1/2 teaspoon ground paprika

1 large handful roughly chopped
  Italian parsley

2 large handfuls roughly chopped
  cilantro leaves

2 garlic cloves

3 tablespoons olive oil

30 mint leaves

1/2 teaspoon soft brown sugar

1 teaspoon salt

Trim the ends off the eggplants and cut the eggplants into 3/4-inch disks. Place in a colander over a bowl and lightly salt. Allow to sit for 30 minutes before rinsing and squeezing dry. Heat the oil in a deep frying pan over medium heat and cook the eggplant rounds in batches until golden, turning once. Drain on paper towels.

To make the harissa, place the roasted bell peppers, cumin, coriander, chilies, paprika, parsley, cilantro, garlic, olive oil, 6 of the mint leaves, the sugar, and the salt in a blender and form a smooth paste. Place 1/2-teaspoon amounts of harissa onto each of the eggplant rounds, top with a fresh mint leaf, and serve.

Note—This mix makes more harissa than you need, but it will keep in the refrigerator in a sealed container for 5 days. Serve with barbecued fish, chicken, or roasted vegetables.

hummus

scant 1¹/₄ cups cooked chickpeas
2 tablespoons lemon juice
3 tablespoons tahini
1 teaspoon ground cumin
1 garlic clove
pinch of cayenne pepper
sea salt and freshly ground black
   pepper, to season
2 tablespoons extra-virgin olive oil

Put the chickpeas, lemon juice, tahini, cumin, garlic, and cayenne pepper into a blender or food processor. Blend to a puree, adding a little water if necessary to make it smooth. Season with sea salt and freshly ground black pepper, then fold the oil through.

watermelon squares

makes 25

1/2 **large seedless watermelon**
1³/4 **ounces feta cheese**
1 **teaspoon sumac**
6 **black olives, seeded and finely sliced**
1¹/2 **tablespoons finely chopped**
  Italian parsley
1 **teaspoon finely chopped thyme**

Cut the watermelon flesh into 1¹/4-inch cubes. Using a melon baller, remove a scoop of watermelon from the top of each cube. Set the cubes aside. Cut the feta into 1/2-inch cubes and place a piece into the top of each watermelon cube. Toss the sumac, sliced olives, parsley, and thyme together in a small bowl, then place a small amount on top of each of the feta squares. Serve immediately.

welsh rarebit

makes 36 squares

2 tablespoons butter
2 tablespoons all-purpose flour
1 teaspoon salt
freshly ground black pepper, to season
2 teaspoons whole-grain mustard
1/2 cup Guinness or stout
1/2 teaspoon Worcestershire sauce
11/4 cups grated mature cheddar
  cheese
9 slices white bread, crusts removed
  and lightly toasted

Preheat the oven to 350°F. Melt the butter in a small saucepan over medium heat and stir in the flour. Add the salt, some freshly ground black pepper, and the mustard. Continue to stir until the mixture begins to turn golden brown. Add the Guinness and Worcestershire sauce and whisk until the mixture is smooth and quite thick. Add three-quarters of the grated cheese and continue to whisk until the cheese melts. Spread thickly onto the slices of toast and sprinkle with the remaining cheese. Place on a baking tray and put in the oven for about 10 minutes. Remove and slice into squares. Serve warm.

chili beef on belgian
endive leaves

serves 4-6

1/2 cup peanut oil

2¹/2-inch piece fresh ginger, peeled
  and julienned

18 ounces ground lean beef

3 large red chilies, seeded and finely
  chopped

2 garlic cloves, crushed

1 teaspoon sesame oil

1 teaspoon balsamic vinegar

2 teaspoons soy sauce

4 tablespoons oyster sauce

10 basil leaves, finely sliced

4 heads Belgian endive, washed and
  leaves separated

Heat the peanut oil in a frying pan over medium–high heat. Add the ginger to the oil and, once it begins to turn crisp and golden, remove and allow to drain on paper towels. Drain most of the oil from the pan, leaving just a little to coat the base, and reduce the heat to medium. Add the beef, chilies, garlic, and sesame oil to the hot pan and stir-fry until the meat is cooked and beginning to brown. Add the vinegar, soy sauce, and oyster sauce. Cook for another 1–2 minutes before adding the basil leaves. Spoon the warm beef mixture into the Belgian endive leaves and top with the fried ginger.

lime and cashew cod rolls

serves 4

1 cup salted, roasted cashew nuts
1 large red chili, seeded and roughly chopped
1 handful cilantro leaves
1 teaspoon finely grated lime zest
1 tablespoon lime juice
18 ounces cod fillets or other firm whitefish fillets, divided into 12 portions
12 small rice paper wrappers
2 tablespoons peanut oil
2 tablespoons Chinese black vinegar or balsamic vinegar

Put the cashews, chili, cilantro, lime zest, and lime juice into a food processor or blender and process into a paste. Put 1 tablespoon of the cashew paste on the top of each fish piece and set aside. Dip one of the rice paper wrappers in a bowl of water until it has softened. Place on a dry surface and put a piece of the fish on top. Fold the wrapper around the fish to form a neat roll. Set aside and repeat with the remaining fish.

Heat half the oil in a nonstick frying pan over medium heat. Cook the fish rolls for 3 minutes on each side or until golden brown. Add more oil when necessary. Serve with the vinegar as a dipping sauce.

gravlax with dill dressing on pumpernickel

makes 30

1 egg yolk
1 teaspoon whole-grain mustard
1 tablespoon lemon juice
1/2 teaspoon sugar
1/2 teaspoon salt
3 tablespoons olive oil
3/4 cup vegetable oil
3 teaspoons finely chopped dill
51/2 ounces gravlax or smoked salmon
30 small slices pumpernickel
freshly ground black pepper, to season

Whisk together the egg yolk, mustard, lemon juice, sugar, and salt in a bowl. Mix the oils together and slowly pour into the egg yolk mixture, whisking continuously until all the oil is mixed through and the dressing thickens. Fold the finely chopped dill through and set aside.

Divide the gravlax or the smoked salmon between the pumpernickel slices and spoon a little of the dressing over the top. Season with freshly ground black pepper and serve.

salt and pepper tofu serves 6-8

1 egg white
2 garlic cloves, crushed
1 teaspoon grated fresh ginger
18 ounces firm tofu, cut into 3/4-inch
  cubes
3 tablespoons sugar
2 teaspoons lime juice
1 teaspoon finely chopped red chili
1/4 cup finely diced cucumber
2 tablespoons finely chopped
  cilantro leaves
1/2 cup cornstarch
1 tablespoon ground Szechuan
  peppercorns
1 teaspoon superfine sugar
1 small red chili, seeded and finely
  chopped
1 tablespoon sea salt
1 teaspoon freshly ground black pepper
1 teaspoon freshly ground white pepper
11/4 cups peanut oil, for panfrying

Whisk the egg white, then add the garlic, ginger, and tofu. Mix well to coat the tofu. Cover and refrigerate overnight.

To make the cucumber sauce, put the sugar and 4 tablespoons of water in a small saucepan and bring to a boil. Cool, then add the lime juice, 1 teaspoon chili, cucumber, and cilantro. Set aside.

In a shallow bowl, mix together the cornstarch, Szechuan pepper, sugar, chili, sea salt, black pepper, and the white pepper.

Heat the oil in a deep frying pan or saucepan over medium heat. Coat the tofu in the flour mixture and shake off any excess. Deep-fry in batches for about 1 minute, or until the tofu is lightly browned. Drain on paper towels. Repeat with the remaining tofu. Serve with the cucumber sauce.

taramasalata

4 thick slices sourdough bread
3$\frac{1}{2}$-ounce can tarama (carp roe)
1 garlic clove, crushed
1 tablespoon diced red onion
3 tablespoons lemon juice
1 cup vegetable oil
warm pita bread, to serve

Soak the sourdough slices in water. Squeeze any excess moisture from the bread and tear it into pieces. Put the bread into a food processor with the tarama, garlic, onion, and lemon juice. Process until smooth, then slowly drizzle in the vegetable oil until it thickens to the consistency of sour cream. Serve with warm pita bread.

spiced pan bread

1 teaspoon sea salt

1/2 cup olive oil

2 garlic cloves, roughly chopped

1 cup sliced scallions

1 teaspoon ground cumin

1 handful Italian parsley

1 tablespoon roughly grated fresh
ginger

1/2 roasted red bell pepper, skin and
seeds removed

1 teaspoon seeded and finely chopped
red chili

2 cups all-purpose flour

2 teaspoons baking powder

2 tablespoons peanut oil

Put the salt, olive oil, garlic, scallions, cumin, parsley, ginger, bell pepper, and chili in a food processor and blend to form a smooth paste. Set aside.

Sift the flour and baking powder into the bowl of a mixer. With the machine running on a low speed, add 4 tablespoons each of hot and cold water. As soon as the dough comes together, transfer to a bowl, cover with plastic wrap, and allow to rest for 15 minutes.

Divide the dough into four pieces. Roll out each piece to form 8-inch rounds. Brush their surfaces with 2 tablespoons of the spicy paste, roll up into logs, then form into spirals. Tuck the tail ends under and flatten the breads. Roll out one of the spirals to form a thin 8-inch circle.

Heat a teaspoon of peanut oil in a frying pan. Cook over medium heat for 4 minutes or until the bottom is golden. Flip and fry the other side. Drain on paper towels. Roll and fry the remaining pieces of dough. Cut into triangles. Serve warm.

sweet-potato chips with
baba ghanoush

serves 6

2 tablespoons olive oil
1 garlic bulb, sliced in half horizontally
1 large eggplant
$1/3$ cup tahini
3 tablespoons lemon juice
sea salt, to season
1 handful finely chopped Italian parsley
1 large orange sweet potato
2 cups vegetable oil
1 teaspoon sumac

Preheat the oven to 400°F. Put the olive oil in a baking dish. Place each garlic half in the dish, cut side down, and add the whole eggplant. Bake for 35–40 minutes, or until the garlic cloves are golden brown and the eggplant is soft. Remove from the oven and allow to cool.

Squeeze the flesh from the roasted garlic and place in a blender or food processor. Cut the eggplant in half, scoop out the flesh, and add to the garlic. Blend until smooth. Transfer to a bowl and fold in the tahini. Add the lemon juice and salt to taste. Fold in the parsley and set aside.

Slice the sweet potato very thinly with a sharp knife or vegetable peeler. Heat the oil in a deep frying pan over medium heat and deep-fry the sweet potato slices, a few at a time, until they are crisp and golden. Drain on paper towels. Sprinkle with sumac and sea salt and serve with the baba ghanoush.

roasted vegetables
with rouille
serves 4

a selection of vegetables such as
  parsnips, onions, fennel, carrots,
  zucchini, winter squash, and sweet
  potatoes to fit into a baking dish
4 tablespoons olive oil
1 thick slice sourdough bread
10 saffron threads
1 red bell pepper, roasted and skinned
1/4 teaspoon ground paprika
1 garlic clove
1/2 cup light olive oil

Preheat the oven to 400°F. Cut the vegetables into large cubes. Put them into a baking dish and rub with the olive oil. Cover with foil and bake for 1 hour.

To make the rouille, tear the bread into pieces and place in a bowl. Bring the saffron threads and 3 tablespoons of water to a boil in a small saucepan and simmer for 1 minute. Soak the bread in the hot saffron water, then put it in a food processor or blender with the bell pepper, paprika, and garlic. Blend to form a smooth paste. Add the light olive oil in a steady stream.

To serve, arrange the vegetables on a serving plate with the rouille.

spiced red cabbage   serves 4

2 tablespoons light olive oil
2 garlic cloves, crushed
1 teaspoon fennel seeds
1 tablespoon mustard seeds
6 cups thinly sliced red cabbage
1/2 cup red wine

Heat the oil in a deep frying pan over medium heat and add the garlic, fennel seeds, and mustard seeds. As the mustard seeds begin to pop, add the cabbage and sauté for a minute. Add the red wine, then cover and simmer over low heat for 30 minutes. Serve with pork sirloin or with any roasted meat.

fennel salad

serves 4

2 tablespoons balsamic vinegar
4 tablespoons olive oil
1 teaspoon Dijon mustard
2 fennel bulbs, finely sliced
2 oranges, segmented
1 large handful Italian parsley
1/4 cup walnuts, roughly chopped
20 niçoise olives

Put the vinegar, oil, and mustard in a small bowl and stir to combine. Toss the fennel, orange, parsley, walnuts, and olives together in a large serving bowl and drizzle with the dressing.

bulgur salad

scant 1 cup bulgur wheat
scant 1/2 cup currants
2 tablespoons olive oil
2 large red onions, finely chopped
1/2 teaspoon ground cinnamon
1/2 teaspoon ground cardamom
1 teaspoon allspice
1 tablespoon grated fresh ginger
2 celery stalks, finely sliced
1 red chili, seeded and finely sliced
1 1/4 cups cooked chickpeas
scant 1/2 cup pine nuts, toasted
sea salt and freshly ground black
  pepper, to season
1 handful cilantro leaves
1 handful Italian parsley
10 mint leaves, roughly chopped

Put the bulgur wheat and currants into a bowl and cover with 1 cup of boiling water. Heat the olive oil in a large saucepan over medium heat. Add the onions, cinnamon, cardamom, allspice, and ginger, and cook until the onion is soft. Lightly fold the onion mixture through the soaked bulgur and currants, along with the celery, chili, chickpeas, and pine nuts. Season with sea salt and freshly ground black pepper.

Spoon into a serving bowl and add the fresh herbs. Serve as a light salad or with broiled chicken.

roasted beet salad

4 large beets
2 short cucumbers, julienned
1/2 red onion, finely diced
2 tablespoons finely chopped dill
1/2 cup light sour cream
2 tablespoons grated fresh horseradish
1 tablespoon lemon juice
salt and pepper, to season
12 cups watercress sprigs, stems
  removed

Preheat the oven to 350°F. Put the unpeeled beets in a roasting pan with 1 cup of water. Cover the pan with foil and bake for 1 hour or until a knife passes easily through the beets. Remove the beets and allow to cool.

Put the cucumbers in a small bowl with the onion and dill and mix together. In a separate bowl, combine the sour cream with the horseradish and lemon juice. Season to taste.

Peel the skins from the beets—they should slip free quite easily. Wear rubber gloves while doing this in case you need to rub the skins off. Cut the beets into thin slices.

Arrange the beets on a serving platter. Top with the cucumber salad and watercress. Gently pour the horseradish dressing over the top, then season and serve.

papaya and coconut sambal

serves 4

2 teaspoons vegetable oil
1 small onion, finely diced
2 tablespoons finely sliced lemongrass,
    white part only
2 teaspoons sambal oelek
1/2 cup dried coconut, toasted
1/2 teaspoon salt
2 teaspoons soft brown sugar
papaya, to serve

Heat the oil in a frying pan over medium heat and cook the onion, lemongrass, and sambal oelek for 5 minutes, stirring occasionally. Reduce the heat to low and add the toasted coconut, salt, and sugar. Cook, stirring regularly, for 12–15 minutes or until golden and crisp. Remove from the heat and allow to cool.

Put the mixture in a food processor and process until it resembles bread crumbs. To serve, slice the papaya into thin wedges and sprinkle with the sambal.

Note—Excess coconut sambal may be stored in an airtight container until needed.

warm banana-chili salad

serves 4

8 banana chilies
4 tablespoons extra-virgin olive oil
1 tablespoon balsamic vinegar
1 teaspoon ground cumin
3 1/2 cups flat green beans
10 large black olives, pitted and
   roughly torn
10 basil leaves, torn

Preheat the oven to 350°F. Put the banana chilies on a baking sheet and bake for 30 minutes, or until the skin begins to blister.

To make the dressing, put the olive oil, vinegar, and cumin in a small bowl and stir to combine.

Blanch the beans in boiling salted water for 2 minutes, or until they turn bright green. Drain and rinse under cold running water.

To serve, cross two of the baked chilies on a plate. Top with the beans, olives, and basil. Drizzle with the dressing.

puy lentil and
spinach salad

serves 4

1 cup Puy lentils
1 teaspoon sea salt
2 oranges
1 tablespoon balsamic vinegar
4 tablespoons extra-virgin olive oil
1 tablespoon Dijon mustard
sea salt and freshly ground black
    pepper, to season
2$1/4$ cups baby spinach leaves
8 red radishes, washed and finely sliced

Put the lentils in a saucepan with 4 cups water and the sea salt. Bring to a boil, reduce the heat, and simmer for 30 minutes. Meanwhile, put the juice and finely grated zest of 1 orange in a large bowl. Add the vinegar, olive oil, and mustard, and stir to combine. When the lentils are tender, drain them of any excess water and add to the bowl. Season to taste with sea salt and freshly ground black pepper.

Zest the remaining orange, slice the skin and pith from it, and cut away the segments. Arrange the spinach, radish, and orange segments in a serving bowl. Then spoon the lentils over the top. Garnish with the remaining orange zest.

fattoush

1 garlic clove, crushed

1 teaspoon sea salt

4 tablespoons lemon juice

4 tablespoons extra-virgin olive oil

3 ripe tomatoes, cut into wedges

2 tablespoons sumac

1 1/2 pieces pita bread

1/2 cup light olive oil

1 long cucumber, peeled, seeded, halved, and thickly sliced

5 scallions, thinly sliced at an angle

6 red radishes, thinly sliced

1 handful baby arugula leaves

1 handful Italian parsley

10 mint leaves, roughly chopped

1 head romaine lettuce, roughly chopped

Put the garlic, salt, lemon juice, and extra-virgin olive oil in a bowl with the tomatoes and sumac and stir together. Slice or tear the pita bread into bite-sized pieces and fry in the light olive oil over medium heat until golden brown. Remove the fried bread with a slotted spoon and drain on paper towels.

Add the cucumber, scallions, radishes, arugula, herbs, and lettuce to the bowl of tomatoes. Toss the fried bread pieces through the fattoush just before serving.

spiced potatoes

4 tablespoons olive oil

3 all-purpose potatoes (about 18 ounces), peeled and diced

2 large red chilies, seeded and finely chopped

3 garlic cloves, crushed

1 teaspoon ground cumin

1/2 teaspoon ground coriander

1/2 teaspoon paprika

salt, to taste

lime wedges, to serve

2 tablespoons lime juice

1 handful cilantro leaves

Heat the olive oil in a heavy-based frying pan over medium heat. Add the potatoes to the oil and stir to coat well. Add the chilies, garlic, spices, and some salt to taste.

Stir the potatoes carefully around the pan until they are soft and golden. Put them on a serving platter with lime wedges, spoon the lime juice over the potatoes, and garnish with the cilantro leaves.

rice with vermicelli, parsley, and puy lentils

serves 4

1/3 cup olive oil
3 garlic cloves, crushed
3 red onions, finely sliced
2 teaspoons ground cumin
1 egg vermicelli nest
11/4 cups basmati rice
1/2 cup Puy lentils
heaping 1 teaspoon sea salt
1 handful Italian parsley,
  roughly chopped
tahini sauce (see basics), to serve

Heat 2 tablespoons of the olive oil in a frying pan and add the garlic, onions, and cumin. Cook over medium heat, stirring occasionally, until the onions are dark brown and caramelized.

Heat the remaining oil in a large saucepan over medium heat. Crush the vermicelli nest in your hands and add to the oil. Stir until the noodles are golden, then add the rice and lentils. Stir together before adding 31/4 cups of water and the sea salt. Bring to a boil, then reduce the heat to low, cover with a lid, and simmer for 20 minutes or until the water is absorbed. Stir in the caramelized onions.

Spoon into a serving bowl. Garnish with the parsley and serve with the tahini sauce. Serve with roasted chicken or spicy sausages.

eggy crepe roll-up

makes 10

sweet bell pepper filling

1 tablespoon olive oil

2 teaspoons ground cumin

1 teaspoon ground coriander

2 teaspoons mustard seeds

2 red onions, diced

2 garlic cloves, finely chopped

1 red bell pepper, diced

1 yellow bell pepper, diced

1 tablespoon balsamic vinegar

sea salt and freshly ground black
    pepper, to season

2 handfuls finely chopped cilantro
    leaves

crepes

1/3 cup finely sliced chives

1 quantity crepe batter (see basics)

3 1/2 tablespoons butter, softened

Heat the oil in a frying pan over high heat and add the cumin, coriander, and mustard seeds. When the mustard seeds begin to pop, add the onion and garlic. Reduce the heat and continue to cook for 5–7 minutes, stirring occasionally, until the onion is transparent. Add the bell peppers, cover and cook for another 15 minutes, stirring occasionally. Add the vinegar and season with salt and freshly ground black pepper.

Stir the chives through the crepe batter. Grease a small frying pan with a little butter and place over medium heat. Add 2 tablespoons of batter and swirl the pan around until the mixture coats the surface of the pan. Cook for a few minutes until the edges of the crepe are crisp, then turn and cook the other side for another minute. Remove from the pan and repeat with the remaining batter.

When all the crepes are cooked, place a heaping tablespoon of the filling in the center of each one, sprinkle with cilantro, and roll up.

steamed eggplant salad

serves 4

1/4 cup tahini

1/4 cup plain yogurt

2 tablespoons lemon juice

2 teaspoons ground cumin

1 garlic clove, crushed

2 eggplants

sea salt and freshly ground black
  pepper, to season

1–2 tablespoons extra-virgin olive oil

1/4 cup toasted pine nuts

1 handful cilantro leaves

1 teaspoon smoked paprika

To make the dressing, put the tahini, yogurt, lemon juice, cumin, and garlic in a bowl. Add 3 tablespoons of water and stir until smooth. Set aside.

Trim the ends off the eggplants. Thinly slice the eggplants widthwise, then place in a steamer. Season with a little sea salt and freshly ground black pepper. Steam for 5–7 minutes or until the eggplant is soft.

Arrange on a serving plate. Drizzle with the dressing and olive oil, and sprinkle with the pine nuts, cilantro, and paprika.

coconut-spiced
sweet potatoes

serves 4

2 medium sweet potatoes, peeled and
cut into bite-sized pieces
1 small cinnamon stick
2 large red chilies, seeded and
finely sliced
finely grated zest of 1 orange
1/2 teaspoon ground nutmeg
14-ounce can coconut milk
buttered couscous (see basics)
cilantro sprigs, to serve
1/2 teaspoon smoked paprika

Put the sweet potatoes, cinnamon stick, chilies, orange zest, nutmeg, and coconut milk in a saucepan with 1 cup water. Bring to a boil, then reduce the heat to a simmer. Cook for 30 minutes or until the sweet potatoes are soft and cooked through.

Serve on a bed of buttered couscous and garnish with cilantro sprigs and a sprinkle of paprika. Serve with chicken or pork.

arugula with baked saffron ricotta

serves 4

2 cups ricotta cheese
pinch saffron threads
2 tablespoons olive oil
sea salt and freshly ground black
   pepper, to season
1 teaspoon balsamic vinegar
3 teaspoons walnut oil
2 fennel bulbs, thinly sliced
10 cups arugula, stalks removed

Preheat the oven to 350°F. Put the ricotta cheese in an ovenproof dish lined with parchment paper. Sprinkle with saffron, drizzle with olive oil, and season with sea salt and freshly ground black pepper. Bake for 30 minutes, then remove from the oven and allow to cool.

Combine the vinegar and walnut oil in a bowl and add the fennel and arugula leaves. Toss together and serve with the baked ricotta.

rice with tomatoes and spinach

serves 6

1 1/2 tablespoons butter

1 large bunch spinach (about
    18 ounces), washed and drained

2 cups basmati rice

3 tablespoons light olive oil

1/2 teaspoon ground turmeric

1 teaspoon ground cumin

1 red onion, finely sliced

2 vine-ripened tomatoes, finely
    chopped

3 cups vegetable stock

Melt the butter in a frying pan over medium heat. Finely chop the spinach and add it to the hot butter. Cover and cook until the spinach is dark green and softly wilted. Remove and set aside. Wash the rice several times until the water runs clear.

In a large saucepan, heat the olive oil over medium heat and add the turmeric, cumin, and onion. Cook for 5–7 minutes, or until the onion is golden and slightly caramelized. Add the rice and stir together for 1 minute.

Squeeze any excess moisture from the spinach, then add it to the rice along with the tomatoes and stock. Stir once, then bring to a boil. Cover, reduce the heat to low, and cook for 25 minutes.

Serve with yogurt, broiled fish, and a wedge of fresh lime.

coconut and ginger pancakes with five-spice duck

makes 20

1 Chinese barbecued duck, skin and flesh shredded

2 teaspoons Chinese five-spice

1 cup rice flour

3/4 teaspoon salt

13/4 cups coconut milk

1 egg, beaten

1 tablespoon shaved jaggery (or brown sugar)

1 teaspoon grated fresh ginger

1–2 tablespoons peanut oil

2 handfuls cilantro leaves

hoisin or plum sauce, for drizzling

Put the duck skin on a baking sheet and broil for 1–2 minutes, or until crisp. Place in a bowl. Add the shredded duck meat and any meat juices, then stir in the five-spice powder.

Make the pancakes by sifting the rice flour and salt into a bowl. Make a well in the center and stir in the coconut milk, egg, jaggery, and ginger. Whisk to form a smooth batter.

Heat the oil in a frying pan over high heat. Place 2–3 cilantro leaves in the center and drizzle 2 tablespoons of the batter over them to form a pancake about 4 inches in diameter. Cook until the edges start to crisp. Turn and cook the other side. Repeat with the remaining batter.

Place a little duck mixture along an end of each pancake. Top with a little hoisin or plum sauce, roll up, and serve.

crab tartlets lentil and fennel sausage salad vietnamese beef soup spicy vegetables with couscous tomato and tofu broth saffron mashed potatoes with roasted beets and mushrooms eggplant and tofu salad calamari salad with red bell pepper and curry vinaigrette braised beef with shiitake mushrooms beet and goat cheese salad ginger duck and udon noodle broth farmer cheese with pomegranate and radicchio

02 light meals

radicchio tamarind duck salad tofu with a black bean sauce wild rice kedgeree red lentil soup eggplant relish with chicken saffron squid and chive salad seared beef slices with plum sauce and mint salad fish and saffron broth skewered swordfish with a spiced

crab tartlets

serves 6

2 cups cherry tomatoes
1 teaspoon chopped thyme
10 saffron threads
scant 2/3 cup light whipping cream
2 egg yolks
2 tablespoons finely chopped chives
6 prebaked 31/4-inch short-crust tartlet
  shells (see basics)
scant 2/3 cup crabmeat
bitter leaf salad, to serve

Preheat the oven to 350°F. Put the cherry tomatoes and thyme in a small baking dish and bake for 20 minutes or until the tomatoes start to split.

Meanwhile, heat the saffron threads with 4 tablespoons water in a small saucepan over high heat until the liquid reduces to 1 tablespoon. Put the saffron liquid in a bowl with the cream, egg yolks, and chives, then whisk together.

Remove the cherry tomatoes from the oven and roughly chop, discarding any tough pieces of skin. Spoon the tomato mixture into the base of the tartlet shells, then divide the crabmeat between them. Ladle the cream mixture into the tart shells. Bake for 15 minutes or until they are just set. Serve with a bitter leaf salad.

tomato and tofu broth

serves 4

4 cups dashi stock (see basics)
2 teaspoons mirin
4 tablespoons white miso paste
1 tablespoon grated fresh ginger
4 plum tomatoes
10½ ounces silken firm tofu
2⅔ cups baby spinach leaves
1 tablespoon soy sauce

Put the dashi stock, mirin, white miso paste, and ginger in a saucepan and bring to a boil. Then reduce the heat to a gentle simmer.

Slice the tomatoes in half and scoop out the seeds using a spoon. Discard the seeds, dice the tomato flesh, and add the tomatoes to the broth. Simmer for an additional 10 minutes.

Cut the tofu into cubes and put it into four soup bowls. Add the spinach leaves and soy sauce to the broth and cook for 1 minute, or until the leaves just wilt. Ladle the soup over the tofu and serve immediately.

eggplant and tofu salad

serves 4

2 tablespoons white miso paste

1 tablespoon soy sauce

1 tablespoon sugar

1 tablespoon sesame oil

3 tablespoons vegetable oil

1 tablespoon finely grated fresh ginger

6 Japanese eggplants, cut into chunks

2 red banana chilies, seeded and cut
  into rings

2 green banana chilies, seeded and cut
  into rings

14 ounces smoked tofu, cut into cubes

1 scallion, finely chopped

1 tablespoon toasted sesame seeds

Mix the miso, soy sauce, and sugar together while slowly adding 1 cup of water.

Heat both the oils together in a large frying pan or wok and add the ginger. As the ginger begins to sizzle, add the eggplant and toss until golden brown. Then pour in the miso and soy mixture and simmer for 10 minutes. Add the banana chilies and cook for an additional 2 minutes, or until they just begin to soften.

Divide the tofu between four plates, top with the eggplant, and garnish with the scallion and sesame seeds.

farmer cheese with pomegranate and radicchio

serves 4

2 tablespoons oil
1 tablespoon brown mustard seeds
1 teaspoon ground cumin
1 red bell pepper, thinly julienned
1 yellow bell pepper, thinly julienned
1 teaspoon sugar
1 small radicchio, leaves washed
7 ounces fresh farmer or goat cheese
1 pomegranate, seeds separated out
  with juice reserved
salt and pepper, to season

Heat the oil in a large frying pan over high heat and add the mustard seeds and ground cumin. As the seeds begin to pop, add the bell peppers and sugar. Toss until the bell peppers begin to soften, then remove the pan from the heat.

To serve, make a bed of radicchio leaves on a plate and top them with the bell peppers. Add a scoop of the cheese and the pomegranate seeds before drizzling with any pomegranate juice. Season well.

braised beef with
shiitake mushrooms   serves 4

12 dried shiitake mushrooms

2 garlic cloves, peeled

2 star anise

1 large red chili, seeded and roughly
    chopped

1 1/4-inch piece fresh ginger, peeled
    and thickly sliced

1 daikon, peeled and cut into 1/2-inch
    thick slices

2 carrots, peeled and sliced

four 5 1/2-ounce beef tenderloin pieces

3 tablespoons soy sauce

3 tablespoons mirin

6 scallions, sliced into 3/4-inch lengths

4 small zucchini, cut diagonally into
    thick slices

Put the shiitake mushrooms into a large bowl and cover with 4 cups hot water. Place a small plate over the mushrooms so they remain covered by the water rather than floating to the surface. Soak for 30 minutes.

Remove the mushrooms from the water and strain the liquid into a large saucepan. Trim the mushrooms of any coarse stalks and put them in the saucepan with the garlic, star anise, chili, ginger, daikon, and carrots. Bring to a boil, then reduce the heat to a simmer and cook for 10 minutes. Add the beef, soy sauce, and mirin. Cover with a lid and continue to simmer slowly for an additional 30 minutes. Add the scallions and zucchini and cook for another 5 minutes.

Serve with the vegetables spooned over the beef, surrounded by a pool of the cooking liquid and a bowl of creamy mashed potatoes or steamed rice on the side.

calamari salad with red bell pepper and curry vinaigrette

serves 4

2 red bell peppers
10 large basil leaves, roughly torn
1 tablespoon lemon juice
1 teaspoon brown sugar
1 teaspoon curry powder
1/3 cup extra-virgin olive oil
salt and pepper, to season
1 tablespoon olive oil
18 ounces small squid, cleaned
2 cups baby spinach leaves

Preheat the oven to 400°F. Roast the bell peppers in the oven, then put them in a plastic bag or covered bowl and allow to cool. When the bell peppers have cooled, peel away the skin and remove the seeds. Finely slice the flesh and place in a large bowl with the basil. Blend together the lemon juice, brown sugar, curry powder, and extra-virgin olive oil, and pour over the bell peppers. Season to taste.

Heat a large frying pan over high heat, add the olive oil, and sear the squid for 2 minutes on each side or until cooked. Slice the squid into thick rings and add it to the bell peppers. Toss the spinach leaves through the salad and season to taste.

tofu with a
black-bean sauce

serves 4

2 tablespoons olive oil

1 tablespoon finely grated fresh ginger

2 garlic cloves, minced

1 teaspoon chili powder

2 tablespoons salted black beans,
   rinsed and drained

3 tablespoons mirin

14 ounces firm tofu, cut into 3/4-inch
   cubes

black pepper, to season

6 zucchini, trimmed and finely sliced
   diagonally

1 lemon, juiced

steamed rice, to serve

Put the olive oil in a large frying pan or wok and heat over high heat. Add the ginger, garlic, and chili powder and stir-fry for 1 minute. Add the black beans, mirin, and 1/2 cup water. Reduce the heat to a simmer, then add the tofu and season with black pepper. Cook for 5 minutes, then add the zucchini. Toss together and cook for an additional 2 minutes before adding the lemon juice. Serve with steamed rice.

vietnamese beef soup serves 4

8 cups beef stock
1 lemongrass stem, crushed
1/4 teaspoon Chinese five-spice
1 tablespoon finely grated fresh ginger
2 red onions, peeled and finely sliced
6 ounces dried rice vermicelli
14 ounces boneless sirloin steak,
    semifrozen and thinly sliced
3 tablespoons fish sauce
1 large handful mint
1 large handful cilantro leaves
1 large handful Vietnamese mint

Put the stock, lemongrass, five-spice powder, ginger, and onions in a large saucepan over high heat and bring to a boil. Reduce the heat and simmer for 10 minutes. Put the rice vermicelli in a large bowl and cover with boiling water. Soak for 5 minutes, then drain and set aside.

Add the steak and fish sauce to the soup. Simmer for 1 minute. Divide the noodles between four bowls. Ladle the hot soup over the top, removing the lemongrass stem. Add a handful of mixed herbs to each bowl and serve.

saffron mashed potatoes with roasted beets and mushrooms

serves 4

8 baby beets

5 1/2 cups mixed matsutake, oyster, and
    fresh shiitake mushrooms

3 tablespoons extra-virgin olive oil

2 garlic cloves, finely sliced

8 thyme sprigs

6 all-purpose potatoes (about 2 1/4
    pounds), peeled and cut into cubes

1/2 cup milk

15 saffron threads

1/2 cup butter

sea salt, to season

4 tablespoons toasted pepitas

Preheat the oven to 400°F. Put the beets in a baking dish with 1/2 cup water. Cover with foil and bake for 1 hour or until cooked. Rub the skin off the cooked beets, then slice in half and wrap in foil. Bake the mushrooms with the olive oil, garlic, and thyme in a baking dish covered with foil for 30 minutes. Just prior to serving, return the mushrooms and beets to the oven to warm.

Meanwhile, cook the potatoes in a saucepan of salted water and drain. Heat the milk, saffron, and butter in a saucepan over medium–low heat until the saffron begins to color the milk. Mash the potatoes while still warm, then whisk in the saffron milk. Season with sea salt.

Cut the warmed beet into quarters and serve with the mashed potatoes and mushrooms. Sprinkle with toasted pepitas and the thyme sprigs from the baking dish.

red lentil soup   serves 4

3 tablespoons olive oil
1 onion, finely diced
1 tablespoon grated fresh ginger
1 tablespoon ground cumin
2 carrots, peeled and grated
1 cup red lentils
4 cups vegetable stock (see basics)
   or water
2 red onions, finely sliced
1 bunch cilantro (about 2 3/4 ounces),
   with roots attached

Put 1 tablespoon of the olive oil in a large saucepan and add the onion, ginger, and cumin. Cook over medium heat until the onion is soft and transparent. Add the carrots, lentils, and stock. Bring the soup to a boil, then reduce to a simmer. Cook for 30 minutes, or until the lentils have completely disintegrated.

Meanwhile, heat the remaining olive oil in a frying pan over medium heat and add the red onions. Thoroughly wash the cilantro. Finely chop the roots and stems, reserving the leaves for garnishing. Add the cilantro roots and stems to the onions and continue to cook, stirring occasionally, until the onion is caramelized.

To serve, ladle the soup into bowls, top with a spoonful of the caramelized onion, and garnish with the reserved cilantro leaves.

wild rice kedgeree   serves 4

1 cup wild rice

pinch sea salt

14-ounce salmon fillet

1 lemon, halved, for squeezing

1 handful Italian parsley

1 handful cilantro leaves

2 vine-ripened tomatoes, cut into
eighths

4 soft-boiled eggs, cut into quarters

curry sauce

4 tablespoons butter

1 red onion, finely diced

1 garlic clove, crushed

2 teaspoons grated fresh ginger

1 teaspoon ground turmeric

1 teaspoon ground cumin

10 saffron threads

1 tablespoon tomato paste

1 cup white wine

Preheat the oven to 350°F. Wash the wild rice in cold water and put it in a saucepan. Cover with 6 cups of water and the pinch of salt. Bring to a boil, then simmer for about 25 minutes. Drain, fluff with a fork, and set aside.

Slice the salmon into four pieces and place in a shallow pan or on a baking sheet. Bake for 5 minutes.

Meanwhile, to make the curry sauce, melt the butter in a heavy-based frying pan, then add the onion, garlic, and ginger. Sauté until the onion is soft and transparent. Add all the spices and sauté for an additional minute. Add the tomato paste and wine and allow to simmer until reduced by half.

Remove the salmon from the oven and squeeze the lemon over the top, then break the salmon into pieces. To assemble, toss the rice with half the herbs and a little of the curry sauce and arrange on plates. Top with the tomatoes, egg, salmon, remaining herbs, and a drizzle of the sauce.

ginger duck and
udon noodle broth

serves 4

8 dried shiitake mushrooms

2 duck breast fillets

8 scallions, trimmed and sliced into
  3/4-inch lengths

2 tablespoons finely grated fresh ginger

7 ounces udon noodles

1 tablespoon dashi granules

4 tablespoons soy sauce

1 tablespoon sugar

7 ounces silken firm tofu, cut into
  3/4-inch cubes

2 tablespoons finely chopped garlic
  chives

Bring a saucepan of salted water to a boil. Put the mushrooms in a bowl and cover with warm water. Soak for 10 minutes, then discard the stalks and finely slice the caps. Return the mushrooms to their soaking liquid.

Trim the fatty skin from the duck and reserve. Cut the breasts diagonally into thin slices. Heat the duck fat in a frying pan over medium heat. Add the scallions, duck breast, and ginger, and sauté lightly for 4–5 minutes. Set aside and discard any fat.

Cook the noodles in the boiling water until al dente, then drain and rinse. Combine the dashi granules, soy sauce, sugar, and 5 cups of water in a saucepan and bring to a boil. Reduce the heat, add the mushrooms and their strained soaking liquid, and simmer for 10 minutes. Add the sautéed duck mixture and tofu and cook for 1 minute.

Divide the noodles between four bowls, ladle the broth over, and serve sprinkled with garlic chives.

beet and goat cheese salad

serves 4-6

4 large beets
1/2 small winter squash, cut into
  bite-sized cubes
3 tablespoons olive oil
salt and pepper, to season
1/2 cup hazelnuts
1 tablespoon balsamic vinegar
1 teaspoon brown mustard seeds
8 cups arugula, stalks removed
7 ounces goat cheese

Preheat the oven to 350°F. Put the unpeeled beets in a roasting pan with 1 cup water. Cover the pan with foil and bake for 1 hour or until a knife passes easily through the beets. Remove the beets and allow to cool.

Toss the squash in 2 tablespoons of the olive oil, season well, and roast for 15 minutes or until pale brown and cooked through. Roast the hazelnuts for 5 minutes, then allow to cool before rubbing away their skins.

Peel the skins from the beets—they should simply slip free. Wear rubber gloves while doing this in case you need to rub the skins off. Slice the beets into eighths lengthwise.

Mix together the vinegar, remaining olive oil, and mustard seeds. Put the beets, squash, hazelnuts, and arugula in a bowl, toss with the dressing, and season. Serve the salad in a bowl with the goat cheese crumbled over.

tamarind duck salad   serves 4

4 duck breasts, thinly sliced across
  the grain
1/2 cup tamarind water (see basics)
2 tablespoons grated fresh ginger
1 teaspoon Chinese five-spice
2 tablespoons shaved jaggery (or
  brown sugar)
11/2 cups snow peas
1 tablespoon sesame oil
1 red bell pepper, julienned
12/3 cups bean sprouts, trimmed
2 tablespoons sesame seeds, toasted

Put the sliced duck, tamarind water, ginger, five-spice, and jaggery in a bowl and leave to marinate for at least 30 minutes.

Blanch the snow peas in boiling water, refresh under cold running water, then slice in half lengthwise.

Heat a wok over high heat. Swirl the sesame oil around the wok and add the duck, reserving the marinade. Stir-fry over high heat for 5 minutes or until cooked. Remove the duck from the heat, allow it to cool a little, then toss in a bowl with the snow peas, bell pepper, and bean sprouts.

Deglaze the wok with the reserved marinade and allow it to simmer for 5 minutes. Pour this over the salad as a dressing and garnish with toasted sesame seeds.

spicy vegetables with couscous

serves 4

1 red onion, cut into eighths
2 garlic cloves, finely sliced
1 cinnamon stick
3/4-inch piece fresh ginger, peeled
  and quartered
1 teaspoon ground paprika
pinch of saffron
13/4 cups canned chopped tomatoes
2 red bell peppers, seeded and cut
  into chunks
1 tablespoon soft brown sugar
21/2 cups cooked chickpeas
3 tablespoons vegetable oil
4 Japanese eggplants, sliced in half
  lengthwise
1 bunch cilantro sprigs, roughly
  chopped
buttered couscous (see basics)

Put the onion, garlic, spices, and tomatoes in a large saucepan, pour in 1 cup of water, and bring to a boil. Add the bell peppers, sugar, and chickpeas, then season and simmer for 30 minutes.

Heat the oil in a frying pan over high heat and fry the eggplant until golden and puffy. Drain on paper towels.

Remove the cinnamon stick and ginger from the chickpea mixture and stir in the cilantro. Serve the eggplant and chickpea mixture on a bed of buttered couscous.

saffron calamari and chive salad

serves 4

10 1/2 ounces orecchiette pasta
3 tablespoons lemon juice
1/2 cup extra-virgin olive oil
1/2 cup chives, chopped into 1/2-inch
  lengths
2 small red chilies, seeded and finely
  chopped
2 tablespoons olive oil
10 saffron threads
1 large red onion, finely diced
6 small squid, cleaned
sea salt and freshly ground black
  pepper, to season
1 handful Italian parsley, roughly
  chopped
2 handfuls baby arugula leaves

Bring a large saucepan of salted water to a boil and cook the pasta until al dente. Drain and set aside.

Meanwhile, put the lemon juice, extra-virgin olive oil, chives, and chilies in a large bowl and stir to combine.

Heat a large nonstick frying pan over medium heat and add the olive oil and saffron. After 1 minute, add the onion and cook until soft and transparent. Remove most of the onion from the pan with a slotted spoon and add it to the dressing in the bowl.

Increase the heat and quickly sauté the squid—they should only need a few minutes on each side. Roughly slice the cooked squid and add to the dressing. Season with sea salt and freshly ground black pepper. Add the pasta and toss together. Pile into a large bowl with the parsley and arugula.

eggplant relish with chicken

4 tablespoons olive oil

10 small Japanese eggplants, sliced
   in half lengthwise

4 red onions, finely sliced

4 garlic cloves, finely sliced

3 tablespoons red wine vinegar

4 tablespoons lemon juice

3 tablespoons soft brown sugar

2 teaspoons white peppercorns,
   lightly crushed

1 handful cilantro leaves

4 skinless, boneless chicken breasts

Preheat the oven to 400°F. Heat the olive oil in a frying pan over medium–high heat. Add the eggplants and fry until golden brown, then remove and put in a large bowl. Add the onions and garlic and, reducing the heat, stir-fry until the onion is soft. Add to the eggplant.

Put the vinegar, lemon juice, sugar, and peppercorns in a saucepan and place over medium heat until the sugar dissolves. Bring to a boil and pour the hot mixture over the eggplant and onion. Stir to combine. Allow to cool, then add the cilantro.

Meanwhile, heat a large frying pan over high heat and sear the chicken until golden brown on both sides. Transfer to a baking sheet and cover with foil. Bake for 15 minutes or until cooked through. Serve with the eggplant relish on the side.

seared beef slices with plum sauce and mint salad

serves 4

4 tablespoons plum sauce
4 tablespoons olive oil
1 tablespoon balsamic vinegar
1/2 teaspoon ground Szechuan
   peppercorns
4 scallions, finely sliced
14 ounces sirloin steak, trimmed
1 1/2 cups bean sprouts, trimmed
1 butter lettuce
1 bunch mint (about 2 3/4 ounces),
   leaves picked
2 tablespoons finely chopped
   cashew nuts

Put the plum sauce, olive oil, vinegar, ground Szechuan peppercorns, and scallions in a bowl. Stir to combine.

Heat a frying pan over high heat and sear the steak for 2 minutes on both sides. Remove from the heat and allow the steak to rest in the pan.

Divide the bean sprouts and lettuce between four plates. Top with a sprinkling of mint leaves. Finely slice the beef and arrange it over the salads. Spoon the plum sauce mixture over the top and sprinkle with the cashews.

fish and saffron broth

1 tablespoon butter
1 large pinch saffron threads
1 onion, finely diced
2 garlic cloves, crushed
1 1/2 inch piece fresh ginger, peeled,
   1 teaspoon finely grated and the
   remainder cut into thin strips
6 ripe plum tomatoes, diced
2 tablespoons tomato paste
1/2 teaspoon sea salt
4 scallions, trimmed and cut into
   1 1/4-inch lengths
eight 4-ounce firm whitefish fillets
1 handful cilantro leaves
crusty bread, to serve

Put the butter, saffron, onion, garlic, and all the ginger into a large heavy-based frying pan and cook over medium heat for 2–3 minutes, until the onion becomes translucent. Add 2 cups water, the tomatoes, tomato paste, and salt. Simmer, covered, for 20 minutes. Add the scallions and fish to the broth and cook covered for 7 minutes.

Divide the fish and broth between four pasta bowls and top with the cilantro. Serve with crusty bread.

skewered swordfish with a spiced tahini sauce
serves 4

1 red onion
1 tablespoon sea salt, plus extra for seasoning
3 lemons
1 teaspoon superfine sugar
1/2 cup tahini
2 tablespoons plain yogurt
1 teaspoon ground cumin
4 swordfish steaks, cut into chunks
3 short cucumbers, thinly sliced diagonally

Soak four wooden skewers in water for 1 hour. Cut the onion in half and finely slice into very thin strips. Put it in a bowl, sprinkle with 1 tablespoon of sea salt, and leave for 20 minutes. Rinse the onion under cold water. Squeeze dry and return to the bowl with the juice of one lemon and the sugar. Toss to combine.

To make the spiced tahini sauce, mix together the tahini with the juice of one lemon, the yogurt, the cumin, and 3 tablespoons of water in a bowl.

Slice the remaining lemon in half lengthwise and then into thick slices. Thread the swordfish and lemon slices onto the soaked skewers. Season with sea salt and set aside. Toss the cucumber and pickled onion together, then divide between four plates.

Heat a large nonstick frying pan over medium–high heat and cook each fish skewer for 2 minutes on each side. Serve with the cucumber salad and spiced tahini sauce.

salad of beets, chickpeas, and feta   serves 4

1³/₄ pounds beets (3–4 beets), leafy
  tops removed
1/2 teaspoon ground cumin
1 orange, juiced
2 tablespoons extra-virgin olive oil
3³/₄ cups wild arugula
2¹/₂ cups canned chickpeas, drained
5¹/₂ ounces marinated feta cheese

Preheat the oven to 400°F. Put the beets into a baking dish with 1/2 cup water. Cover with foil and bake for 1 hour or until a knife passes easily through the beets. Remove and allow to cool. Peel the skins from the beets—they should slip free quite easily. Wear rubber gloves while doing this in case you need to rub the skins off. Cut the beets into small wedges and place in a bowl. Add the cumin, orange juice, and olive oil. Toss to ensure the beet is coated in the dressing.

Arrange the arugula, dressed beets, chickpeas, and marinated feta on a serving dish and drizzle with any remaining beet dressing.

spiced carrot soup

serves 4

3¹/₂ tablespoons butter
1 red onion, diced
1 teaspoon ground cumin
¹/₄ cup red lentils
4 carrots, peeled and finely chopped
4 cups vegetable stock (see basics)

Put the butter into a saucepan over medium heat and add the onion and cumin. Cook until the onion is soft and transparent, then add the lentils and carrots. Stir for 1 minute, then add the vegetable stock. Bring to a boil, then reduce the heat to a slow simmer. Continue to cook for 40 minutes or until the carrot is soft and beginning to fall apart. Remove from the heat and allow to cool.

Put the soup into a food processor or blender a few ladles at a time and blend to a smooth puree. Return to a clean saucepan and heat over low heat when ready to serve.

szechuan eggplant   serves 4

1 cup vegetable oil
2 small eggplants, cut into cubes
2 large red chilies, seeded and finely
  sliced
1 teaspoon roasted Szechuan
  peppercorns, ground
2 garlic cloves, finely chopped
1¹/₂ tablespoons finely grated fresh
  ginger
4 scallions, sliced diagonally
3 tablespoons light soy sauce
1 tablespoon balsamic vinegar
1 teaspoon sugar

Heat the oil in a wok or a deep saucepan and deep-fry the eggplant in batches until golden brown. Remove the eggplant using a slotted spoon and drain on paper towels. Pour most of the oil out of the wok, leaving behind 1 tablespoon.

Reheat the oil and add the chilies, ground peppercorns, garlic, ginger, and scallions. Stir-fry for 30 seconds. Add the fried eggplant, soy sauce, vinegar, and sugar, then stir-fry for an additional minute. Serve with buckwheat or somen noodles.

roasted winter squash and quinoa salad

serves 4

1 winter squash (about 2 1/4 pounds),
  seeds removed and peeled
2 tablespoons olive oil
freshly ground black pepper, to season
2 red bell peppers
1/2 cup quinoa
3 cups arugula leaves
harissa (see basics), to serve

Preheat the oven to 350°F. Cut the squash into 3/4-inch thick wedges and place on a baking sheet lined with parchment paper. Rub the olive oil over the squash and season with freshly ground black pepper. Cut the bell peppers into 3/4-inch squares and place on another lined baking sheet. Bake the squash and bell peppers for 20 minutes. Remove the bell peppers from the oven and set aside. Turn the squash wedges over, then return to the oven for an additional 20 minutes.

Rinse the quinoa in a small strainer under cold running water. Drain and place in a saucepan with 1 cup cold water. Bring to a boil. Reduce to a simmer, cover, and cook until all the water is absorbed. Drain.

Remove the squash from the oven and divide between four warm plates. Add the arugula leaves, baked bell peppers, and quinoa. Serve with a dollop of harissa.

mexican spiced
chili beans

serves 4

2 tablespoons olive oil
1 onion, finely diced
2 garlic cloves, crushed
1 1/2 teaspoons smoked paprika
2 teaspoons ground cumin
1/2 teaspoon oregano
18 ounces ground pork
1 tablespoon tomato paste
1 cup red wine
1 3/4 cups canned chopped tomatoes
1 1/3 cups canned kidney beans
20 kalamata olives, pitted and roughly
  chopped
sour cream, cilantro leaves, and crispy
  flat bread, to serve

Put the olive oil in a large saucepan with the onion, garlic, paprika, cumin, and oregano. Cook over medium heat until the onion is soft, then add the ground pork. Sauté until the pork is cooked through and beginning to break up. Add the tomato paste, wine, and tomatoes, and stir to combine. Simmer over low heat for 40 minutes, then add the kidney beans and olives. Cook for another 10 minutes before spooning into warm bowls. Top with sour cream, sprinkle with cilantro leaves, and serve with crispy flat bread.

lentil and fennel sausage salad

1 cup Puy lentils
1 teaspoon sea salt
1 tablespoon balsamic vinegar
4 tablespoons extra-virgin olive oil
1 tablespoon whole-grain mustard,
  plus extra to serve
8 fennel sausages
1/2 red onion, thinly sliced
1 cup croutons (see basics)
1 large handful Italian parsley

Put the lentils in a saucepan with 4 cups water and the sea salt. Bring to a boil, reduce the heat, and simmer for 30 minutes or until tender. Drain the lentils of any excess water, then stir in the vinegar, 2 tablespoons olive oil, and the mustard.

Fry the sausages in a frying pan until they are cooked through.

Toss the onion, croutons, and parsley with the lentils, divide between four plates, and drizzle with a little more olive oil. Top with the sausages and serve with a dollop of extra mustard.

thyme and sumac-seared tuna with minted potatoes

serves 4

1 1/4 pounds fingerling or new potatoes
sea salt, for boiling
1 tablespoon finely chopped thyme
3 tablespoons finely chopped chives
3 tablespoons sumac
18-ounce tuna fillet, cut into smaller
  fillets
2 tablespoons olive oil
1/2 cup extra-virgin olive oil
1 tablespoon lemon juice
1 handful mint
salt and pepper, to season

Put the potatoes in a saucepan of cold water with some sea salt and bring to a boil over high heat. When the water reaches the boiling point, cover with a lid and remove from the heat. Leave the potatoes to sit for 30 minutes. Put the thyme, chives, and sumac on a plate and roll the tuna in the herbs until each fillet is covered.

Heat a frying pan over high heat and add the 2 tablespoons of olive oil. Sear the tuna fillets for 2 minutes on each side. Remove the pan from the heat. Allow the tuna to sit in the pan until ready to serve.

To make the dressing, mix together 4 tablespoons of the extra-virgin olive oil and the lemon juice in a bowl. Drain the potatoes and return them to the saucepan. Using a spoon, break up the potatoes and add the remaining extra-virgin olive oil. Season well.

Slice the tuna into bite-sized pieces and serve on top of the potatoes. Scatter with the mint leaves and drizzle with the dressing.

seared snapper with spiced butter lamb fillet with cumin and tomato spiced barramundi Cajun-roasted turkey fish tagine cider-glazed pork sirloin spiced tomato and shrimp honeyed duck breast with chinese cabbage chermoula kingfish quince and red wine duck cashew curry broiled chicken with aioli thyme and sumac-seared tuna with minted potatoes rice with tomatoes and spinach seared lamb on ginger lentils

03 main meals

chicken curry braised eggplant with water chestnuts spiced ocean trout chili mint lamb with saffron vegetables baked leeks with seared salmon spiced pork with warm greens baked salmon with hijiki and radish salad moroccan lamb chipotle chicken spice

potato, bell pepper, and zucchini curry

serves 4

18 ounces new potatoes, sliced in half
3 tablespoons olive oil
2 large red onions, halved and sliced
  into eighths
2 garlic cloves, crushed
1 teaspoon ground turmeric
1 tablespoon grated fresh ginger
1 teaspoon fennel seeds, lightly crushed
3 red chilies, seeded and finely chopped
14-ounce can coconut milk
1 red bell pepper, cut into thick strips
5 Kaffir lime leaves
5 zucchini (about 18 ounces), sliced
4 tablespoons lime juice
2 teaspoons fish sauce
3 handfuls cilantro leaves

Put the potatoes in a saucepan and cover with cold water. Bring to a boil, cover, and remove from the heat.

Meanwhile, heat the olive oil in a saucepan over medium heat. Add the onions, garlic, turmeric, ginger, fennel seeds, and chilies. Cook until the onions are soft, then add the coconut milk, bell pepper, and lime leaves. Add the strained potatoes, cover, and simmer for 15 minutes. Add the zucchini and cook for an additional 5 minutes. When ready to serve, add the lime juice and fish sauce. Garnish with cilantro leaves.

seared snapper with spiced butter

1/3 cup butter, softened
1 onion, finely diced
1 tablespoon brown mustard seeds
1 teaspoon cayenne pepper
1 teaspoon curry powder
1 small handful finely chopped
  cilantro leaves
four 6-ounce snapper fillets
1 tablespoon vegetable oil
steamed green beans, lime wedges,
  and mixed leaf salad, to serve

Put 1 1/2 tablespoons of the butter in a frying pan over medium heat and add the diced onion. Sauté until the onion is soft and lightly golden. Add the mustard seeds, cayenne pepper, and curry powder, and cook for an additional 2 minutes. Remove from the heat and set aside to cool. When the onion mixture has cooled, fold in the remaining butter and cilantro.

Rinse the snapper fillets in cold water and pat dry with paper towels.

Heat the oil in a frying pan over high heat and add the snapper fillets, skin side down. Fry for several minutes until the skin is lightly browned, then flip the fish over and cook the other side for an additional 2–3 minutes, depending on the thickness of the fillet. Serve on a bed of steamed green beans with the spiced butter, some lime wedges, and a mixed leaf salad.

lamb fillet with cumin and tomato

serves 4

2 large ripe tomatoes, cut into eighths
1/2 tablespoon sea salt
1 teaspoon ground cumin
1 tablespoon olive oil
1 red onion, halved and cut
  into wedges
1 tablespoon vegetable oil
18 ounces lamb tenderloin, trimmed
2 cups spinach leaves
freshly ground black pepper, to season

Preheat the oven to 350°F. Put the tomatoes in a roasting pan and sprinkle with the salt, cumin, olive oil, and onion. Roast for 20 minutes.

When the tomatoes are almost ready, heat an ovenproof frying pan over high heat and add the vegetable oil. Sear the lamb fillet on all sides until it is well browned, then transfer to the oven for 5–8 minutes, depending on how well done you like it. Remove the tomatoes and lamb from the oven.

Divide the spinach leaves between four plates and top with the tomato. Slice the lamb against the grain into thin slices, arrange over the tomatoes, drizzle with the pan juices, and season with freshly ground black pepper.

fish tagine

serves 4

4 tablespoons olive oil

1 large red onion, roughly chopped

10 saffron threads

1 teaspoon ground cumin

4 large all-purpose potatoes, sliced
  into bite-sized pieces

2 celery stalks, roughly chopped

1³/₄ cups canned chopped tomatoes

1 small cinnamon stick

1¹/₄ pounds thick snapper fillets, cut
  into 1¹/₂-inch chunks

sea salt and freshly ground black
  pepper, to season

1 handful Italian parsley

2 tablespoons finely chopped
  preserved lemon

crusty bread, to serve

Heat the olive oil in a large, deep frying pan or casserole pot over medium heat. Add the onion, saffron, and cumin, and cook until the onion is soft and slightly caramelized. Add the potatoes, celery, tomatoes, cinnamon, and 1 cup water. Bring to a boil, then reduce the heat to a simmer and cook for 10 minutes.

When the potatoes are soft, season the fish fillets with sea salt and add them to the stew. Simmer for an additional 10 minutes, then season with freshly ground black pepper. Garnish with the parsley leaves and preserved lemon, and serve with warm crusty bread.

spiced fish fillets   serves 4

12 whole macadamia nuts

1/4 white onion, finely diced

4 garlic cloves

2 red chilies, seeded and finely
    chopped

2 teaspoons finely grated fresh ginger

1 teaspoon ground turmeric

4 tablespoons tamarind water
    (see basics)

1 teaspoon soy sauce

four 7-ounce firm whitefish fillets

1/2 cup coconut milk

steamed Asian greens, to serve

Preheat the oven to 400°F. Whiz the macadamia nuts, onion, garlic, chilies, ginger, turmeric, tamarind water, and soy sauce to a paste in a blender or food processor. Rinse the fish fillets in cold water and pat dry with paper towels. Rub half the paste over the fish, put it on a baking sheet, and bake for 12 minutes.

Put the remaining paste in a small saucepan and add the coconut milk. Stir over medium heat.

Serve the fish with steamed Asian greens and the spicy coconut milk.

cajun-roasted turkey   serves 4

2¼ pounds spinach
1 boneless turkey breast (about
   2¾ pounds)
1 tablespoon olive oil
2 tablespoons sweet Cajun spice mix
sea salt and freshly ground black
   pepper, to season
¾ cup thyme sprigs
cranberry sauce, to serve

Preheat the oven to 350°F. Blanch the spinach in boiling water, then drain.

Cut into the turkey breast to make a pocket for the spinach, then rub it with the oil and Cajun spice mix. Put the turkey onto a sheet of parchment paper large enough to wrap around it. Squeeze any excess moisture from the spinach and stuff it into the pocket. Season the turkey with sea salt and freshly ground black pepper and cover with a sprinkling of thyme sprigs. Wrap the paper around the turkey and secure with cooking twine. Place the turkey on a baking sheet and bake for 40 minutes.

Remove the turkey from the oven and reserve any of the juices. Slice the turkey, divide between warm serving plates, and pour over the reserved liquid. Serve with cranberry sauce.

cashew curry

2 onions, diced
3 garlic cloves, crushed
1 1/2-inch piece fresh ginger, chopped
1 tablespoon olive oil
1 teaspoon turmeric
1 small cinnamon stick
6 curry leaves
1 lime, juiced
3 red bell peppers, cut into
   1/2-inch squares
1 2/3 cups cashew nuts
14-ounce can coconut milk
2 large red chilies, seeded and finely
   chopped
2 handfuls cilantro leaves
steamed basmati rice, to serve

Put the onion, garlic, and ginger in a food processor and process to form a paste.

Heat the olive oil in a heavy-based saucepan over medium heat and add the onion paste. Cook for 5 minutes. Add the turmeric, cinnamon stick, curry leaves, and lime juice, and cook for 2–3 minutes. Add the bell peppers and cashews. Stir, then add the coconut milk and 1 cup water. Simmer for 1 hour.

Transfer the curry into a large serving bowl and top with the chilies and cilantro leaves. Serve with steamed basmati rice.

cider-glazed pork sirloin

serves 6

2 cups apple cider

1/4 cup honey

3 garlic cloves, peeled and finely
  chopped

3 star anise

1 cinnamon stick

1 large red chili, split in half

2 bay leaves

21/4-pound pork sirloin, skin
  cut off and reserved

salt, for sprinkling

3 green apples, peeled, cored, and
  thickly sliced

1 tablespoon balsamic vinegar

Put the cider, honey, garlic, star anise, cinnamon stick, chili, and bay leaves in a bowl. Cut slashes diagonally over the pork, then add the pork to the marinade, coating it all over. Cover and refrigerate overnight.

Preheat the oven to 400°F. Reserving the marinade, put the pork in a roasting pan, cover with foil, and roast for 40 minutes. To make the crackling, score the reserved pork skin with a sharp knife and cut into several strips. Put the strips in a roasting pan and brush with water. Sprinkle with salt. Roast for 20 minutes or until the skin is golden brown. Drain off any fat.

Put the apples in a saucepan with 1/2 cup of the marinating liquid. Bring to a boil and then leave to simmer for 15 minutes. Add the vinegar and season well.

Uncover the pork and baste it with the pan juices. Cook for an additional 20 minutes or until the juices run clear when a skewer is inserted into the meat. Allow the pork to sit for 10 minutes before carving. Serve with the apple relish and crackling.

honeyed duck breast with chinese cabbage

serves 4

4 duck breasts
1 teaspoon Chinese five-spice
1 teaspoon salt
3 tablespoons butter
8 cups finely sliced Chinese cabbage
2 tablespoons honey
2 oranges, juiced

Preheat the oven to 400°F. Score the skin of the duck breasts in a crisscross pattern and rub the five-spice powder into the skin along with the salt.

Melt the butter in a frying pan over medium heat. Add the cabbage, then sauté for several minutes, or until the cabbage is soft and transparent. Season and reduce the heat to low.

Drizzle the honey over the duck breasts and roast for 15 minutes. Check that the breasts are cooked through, allow to rest for 1 minute covered with foil, and then slice thinly.

Serve the duck with the cabbage and a drizzle of fresh orange juice.

chermoula kingfish   serves 4

1 tablespoon cumin seeds, roasted
1 tablespoon coriander seeds, roasted
1 tablespoon ground paprika
1 tablespoon freshly grated ginger
2 garlic cloves
1 roasted red bell pepper, seeded and
    skin removed
4 tablespoons roughly chopped
    cilantro leaves
2 tablespoons olive oil
four 6½-ounce kingfish fillets (cod
    or a similar meaty fish can also
    be used)
sea salt, to season
lime wedges, to serve
mashed potatoes (see basics), to serve

Preheat the oven to 400°F. Put all the spices in a food processor with the garlic, roasted bell pepper, cilantro, and olive oil, and process to a thick paste (or use a mortar and pestle).

Rub the paste over the fish fillets. Place the fish, skin side up, on a baking sheet and season with sea salt. Bake for 12 minutes. Remove from the oven and check with the point of a small knife that the fish is cooked through. Serve with lime wedges and creamy mashed potatoes.

braised eggplant with water chestnuts

4 tablespoons olive oil
2 large red chilies, seeded and finely
  chopped
2 garlic cloves, minced
1 tablespoon finely grated fresh ginger
4 scallions, trimmed and cut into
  3/4-inch lengths
2 eggplants, cut into 3/4-inch squares
11/3 cups canned water chestnuts,
  drained
2 cups vegetable stock (see basics)
1 tablespoon soy sauce
1 tablespoon balsamic vinegar
11/2 cups snap peas
steamed white rice, to serve

Heat the olive oil in a wok or large frying pan over high heat. Add the chilies, garlic, and ginger, and stir-fry for 1 minute. Add the scallions and eggplant, and cook for an additional 5 minutes, or until the eggplant is soft and golden brown. Add the water chestnuts, vegetable stock, soy sauce, and balsamic vinegar, and reduce the heat to a simmer. Simmer until the liquid has reduced by half.

Meanwhile, blanch the snap peas in boiling water until bright green. Drain and rinse under cold running water. Add the peas to the braised eggplant and cook for an additional minute. Serve with steamed white rice.

broiled chicken
with aioli

serves 4

4 chicken leg quarters
1 tablespoon finely chopped thyme
2 tablespoons ground cumin
1 teaspoon ground coriander
1 teaspoon ground paprika
1 teaspoon sea salt
1 lemon, juiced
4 tablespoons olive oil
green salad, to serve
aioli (see basics), to serve

Put the chicken pieces into a large bowl and add the thyme, cumin, coriander, paprika, and sea salt. Rub the spices into the skin and then drizzle the lemon juice and olive oil over the chicken. Cover and marinate in the refrigerator for a few hours or overnight.

Preheat the oven to 425°F. Heat a barbecue grill plate to medium and cook the chicken for 2–3 minutes on each side. Transfer to a baking dish and bake in the oven for 35 minutes or until cooked through.

Serve with a green salad and a dollop of aioli.

spiced tomato and shrimp

serves 4

1 tablespoon light olive oil
1/2 teaspoon cumin seeds
2 large green chilies, seeded and
  finely chopped
1/2 teaspoon ground turmeric
2 cups cherry tomatoes, sliced in half
16 large raw shrimp, peeled and
  deveined with tails intact
1/2 cup coconut milk
sea salt and freshly ground black
  pepper, to serve
1 handful Thai basil, to garnish
steamed white rice, to serve

Heat the olive oil in a frying pan over high heat and add the cumin seeds, chilies, and turmeric. Reduce the heat to medium after 1 minute, add the tomatoes, and cook for an additional minute. Add the shrimp and cook for 2–3 minutes on each side or until they are pink on both sides and beginning to curl up. Remove the shrimp and set aside. Add the coconut milk to the pan, season with sea salt and freshly ground black pepper, then stir and simmer for 1 minute.

Meanwhile, arrange the shrimp on four plates. Spoon the coconut milk over the top and garnish with Thai basil leaves. Serve with steamed white rice.

summer spiced trout

1¹/₄ pounds ocean trout fillet, skin and
   bones removed
1 teaspoon sesame oil
4 scallions, trimmed and cut into
   1¹/₄-inch lengths
³/₄ cup cider vinegar
¹/₄ cup sugar
³/₄-inch piece fresh ginger, peeled
   and julienned
2 large red chilies, seeded and finely
   sliced
4-inch piece young lemongrass,
   finely chopped
4 star anise
1 teaspoon Szechuan peppercorns
udon noodles, to serve

Cut the fish into ¹/₂-inch-wide slices and put them in a single layer in a large, deep, nonmetallic dish.

Put the sesame oil and scallions in a saucepan over medium heat and cook until the scallions have turned bright green. Pour in 2 cups of water and stir in the vinegar, sugar, ginger, chilies, lemongrass, star anise, and peppercorns. Bring to a boil, stirring to make sure that the sugar has dissolved, then pour the hot liquid over the trout and allow to cool. Serve with udon noodles.

chicken curry

4 tablespoons olive oil

2 large red onions, finely sliced

2 garlic cloves, finely chopped

2 tablespoons grated fresh ginger

1 teaspoon ground turmeric

3 plum tomatoes, roughly chopped

2 red bell peppers, cut into 3/4-inch
   squares

10 curry leaves

14-ounce can coconut milk

three 7-ounce skinless, boneless
   chicken breast fillets, cut into
   thick strips

salt and pepper, to season

3 limes, juiced

1 bunch (about 23/4 ounces) cilantro
   sprigs, roughly chopped

steamed white rice, to serve

Heat the oil in a large saucepan over medium heat and add the onions and garlic. Cook for 3 minutes, then stir in the ginger and turmeric. Cook for an additional minute before adding the tomatoes, bell peppers, curry leaves, coconut milk, and chicken. Simmer for 30 minutes, then season to taste. Add the lime juice and cilantro, and serve with steamed white rice.

seared lamb
on ginger lentils

2 tablespoons olive oil
1 red onion, finely diced
2 garlic cloves, crushed
3 tablespoons grated fresh ginger
1 teaspoon ground cumin
1 cup red lentils
2 lamb fillets (about 18 ounces),
   trimmed
salt and pepper, to season
1 orange, zested and juiced
extra-virgin olive oil, for drizzling
cilantro leaves, roughly chopped,
   to garnish

Preheat the oven to 350°F. Heat the oil in a saucepan over medium heat and add the onion and garlic. Cook for 1–2 minutes or until the onion starts to soften. Add the ginger, cumin, and lentils. Stir for 1–2 minutes or until the lentils are glossy and well coated. Pour in 2 1/2 cups water, then simmer for 30 minutes, or until the lentils are soft.

Sear the lamb on both sides, then roast in the oven for 5 minutes. Remove the lamb from the oven, season, cover with foil, and allow to rest for 1 minute before carving.

Stir the orange zest and juice into the hot lentils. Season, then spoon into four bowls and top with slices of lamb. Season to taste. Drizzle with the pan juices and a little extra-virgin olive oil, and garnish with cilantro leaves.

quince and red wine duck

serves 4

12 thyme sprigs
1 cup red wine
2 garlic cloves, sliced in half
4 duck breast fillets
3 tablespoons quince paste
1 teaspoon cumin
sea salt and freshly ground black
  pepper, to season
buttered couscous (see basics),
  to serve

Preheat the oven to 400°F. Arrange the thyme sprigs over the base of a baking dish to form a bed for the duck. Add the wine and garlic to the dish. Rinse the duck fillets under cold running water and pat dry with paper towels. With a sharp knife, make several incisions through the fatty skin on each of the fillets. Rub the quince paste into the skin, sprinkle with the cumin, and season with sea salt and freshly ground black pepper.

Place the duck fillets on top of the thyme, flesh side down. Bake for 5 minutes, then remove from the oven and spread the softened quince paste over the fillets with a knife. Return to the oven for an additional 10 minutes. For crispy skin, put the cooked duck under a hot broiler for 2 minutes. Allow to sit for a few minutes, then slice. Serve with buttered couscous, a few thyme sprigs, and a spoonful of the cooking liquid drizzled over.

chili mint lamb with saffron vegetables

serves 4

3 tablespoons olive oil

2 tablespoons harissa (see basics)

1 bunch mint (about 2³/₄ ounces),
  leaves removed and finely chopped

1 large handful cilantro (leaves,
  finely chopped)

4 French-trimmed lamb racks

sea salt and freshly ground black
  pepper, to season

3 onions, peeled and quartered

3 parsnips, peeled and cut into cubes

4 waxy potatoes, peeled and cut
  into cubes

1³/₄ pounds winter squash, peeled and
  cut into cubes

1 teaspoon sugar

¹/₂ teaspoon crushed fennel seeds

20 black olives, pitted

1 teaspoon ground cumin

10 saffron threads

3 tablespoons lemon juice

Preheat the oven to 425°F. In a bowl, mix together 2 tablespoons of the olive oil, the harissa, and the herbs. Rub the mixture into the lamb, then season with sea salt and freshly ground black pepper.

Place the vegetables in a baking dish and toss with the remaining olive oil, sugar, fennel seeds, olives, cumin, saffron, and lemon juice. Cover with foil and bake for 30 minutes, then turn the vegetables and return uncovered to the oven.

Sear the lamb in a frying pan over high heat, then place it on top of the vegetables and bake for 20 minutes. Rest the lamb for 2–3 minutes, slice, and serve with the vegetables.

baked leeks
with seared salmon
serves 4

3 leeks, washed
4 scallions, trimmed
10 saffron threads
1 tablespoon salted capers
2 tablespoons butter
1 tablespoon olive oil
four 5 1/2-ounce salmon fillets, skin on
2 handfuls baby spinach leaves

Preheat the oven to 350°F. Cut the leeks and scallions into short lengths and put them in a baking dish with the saffron, capers, butter, and 3/4 cup of water. Cover with foil and bake for 1 hour.

Heat a nonstick frying pan over high heat and add the olive oil. Sear the salmon, skin side down, for 2 minutes, then turn over. Cover, reduce the heat, and cook for an additional 3 minutes. Divide the spinach leaves between four plates. Top with the salmon and spoon over the baked leeks.

spiced pork with
warm greens

serves 4

2 tablespoons soy sauce
2 tablespoons mirin
1 tablespoon sesame oil
2 garlic cloves, crushed
1 tablespoon brown sugar
1 teaspoon Chinese five-spice
4 star anise
1 tablespoon finely grated fresh ginger
2 small pork sirloin fillets
3 bunches (about 2³⁄4 pounds) choy
  sum, washed
steamed rice, to serve

Put the soy sauce, mirin, sesame oil, garlic, sugar, five-spice, star anise, and ginger in a large bowl. Stir until the sugar has dissolved and the ingredients are combined. Add the pork fillets, turn to coat, then cover and refrigerate overnight.

Preheat the oven to 350°F. Heat a nonstick frying pan over high heat and add the pork, reserving the marinade. Sear on both sides until golden, then transfer to a baking sheet and bake for 10 minutes. Pour the remaining marinade into the frying pan with 1/2 cup water. Simmer for 3 minutes.

Meanwhile, steam or stir-fry the choy sum until bright green. Remove the pork from the oven and allow to rest for a few minutes.

Serve thin slices of pork with the warm greens, steamed rice, and a spoonful of the sauce.

baked salmon with arame and radish salad

serves 4

2 tablespoons arame or hijiki
6 umeboshi plums, seeds removed
4 tablespoons mirin
2 teaspoons sesame oil
four 7-ounce salmon fillets, skin on
2 tablespoons vegetable oil
2 1/2 cups julienned daikon
1 tablespoon finely sliced pickled
   ginger
1 tablespoon pickled ginger juice
14 ounces watercress, leaves only

Preheat the oven to 350°F. Soak the arame in warm water for 20 minutes. Mash the plums until they are soft, then add the mirin and sesame oil.

Rinse the salmon fillets in cold water and pat them dry with paper towels. Rub the plum glaze into the flesh of the fish.

Heat the vegetable oil in an ovenproof frying pan over high heat and add the salmon fillets, skin side down. Sear the fish for a few minutes, then put the pan in the oven and bake the fish for 10 minutes.

Meanwhile, toss the arame, daikon, ginger, and ginger juice together in a bowl with the watercress leaves. Pile the mixture onto four plates and top with the salmon fillets.

moroccan lamb   serves 4

1/2 cup lemon juice
3 tablespoons olive oil
1 teaspoon ground cinnamon
3 garlic cloves, sliced
1 teaspoon ground cumin
zest of 1 orange, finely grated
2 lamb fillets, trimmed (about
   18 ounces)
1 handful Italian parsley
20 mint leaves, roughly chopped
20 oregano leaves
2 vine-ripened tomatoes, roughly
   chopped
buttered couscous (see basics),
   to serve

Mix together the lemon juice, olive oil, cinnamon, garlic, cumin, and orange zest in a glass or ceramic bowl. Add the lamb, turn to coat, then cover and refrigerate for 3 hours or overnight.

Remove the lamb from the marinade and sear in a nonstick frying pan over high heat. Cook until the uncooked side begins to look a little bloody, then turn the fillets over. Reduce the heat and cook for an additional 5 minutes. Allow to rest for a few minutes.

Toss the herbs and tomatoes together in a bowl and divide between four plates. Slice the lamb across the grain and arrange over the tomato salad. Serve with buttered couscous.

chipotle chicken serves 4

1 teaspoon allspice
1/2 teaspoon cinnamon
1 teaspoon ground cumin
1 teaspoon ground coriander
1 tablespoon canned chipotle chili,
  finely chopped
2 tablespoons oregano leaves
4 tablespoons olive oil
2 tablespoons lime juice
4 chicken drumsticks
4 chicken thighs
1 orange, zested and juiced
1 3/4 cups canned tomatoes
2 green bell peppers, cut into thick
  cubes
buttered couscous (see basics),
  to serve
lime halves, cilantro leaves, and
  chopped green olives, to serve

Put the allspice, cinnamon, cumin, coriander, chipotle chili, oregano, olive oil, and lime juice in a large bowl and stir together. Add the chicken pieces and toss until well coated. Cover and marinate in the refrigerator for a few hours or overnight.

Heat a large frying pan over high heat. Add the chicken and cook until golden brown. Set aside on paper towels.

Drain any excess fat from the pan and add the orange zest and juice, tomatoes, bell peppers, and chicken. Cover and simmer for 30 minutes. Serve on a bed of buttered couscous with lime halves, cilantro, and chopped green olives.

spice-crusted fish
serves 4

2 tablespoons coriander seeds
2 tablespoons cumin seeds
1¹/₂ tablespoons sea salt
freshly ground black pepper, to taste
1 garlic clove
2 large handfuls Italian parsley
2 tablespoons extra-virgin olive oil
four 7-ounce cod or other firm
   whitefish fillets
2 tablespoons light olive oil
mashed potatoes (see basics), to serve
lemon wedges, to serve

Preheat the oven to 350°F. Place the coriander and cumin seeds on a baking sheet and roast for 2 minutes or until they begin to darken. Remove, cool briefly, and put in a mortar and pestle or spice grinder with the salt and some freshly ground black pepper. Grind to a powder, then add the garlic, parsley, and extra-virgin olive oil. Work the seasoning to a paste.

Rinse the fish in cold water and pat dry with paper towels. Pat the paste onto the top of each fish fillet, forming a thick crust that completely covers the surface.

Heat the light olive oil in a large ovenproof frying pan over high heat until it begins to shimmer. Add the fish to the pan, crust side down. Sear for 1 minute, turn over, and cook for an additional minute. Put the pan in the oven for 5 minutes. Remove the fish and serve on a bed of mashed potatoes with lemon wedges.

beef fillet with horseradish and garlic butter

serves 6

3¹/₄-pound beef tenderloin
2 tablespoons freshly ground
  black pepper
3 garlic bulbs
3 tablespoons butter
2 teaspoons grated fresh horseradish
  or horseradish sauce
salt and pepper, to season
sautéed baby carrots, to serve
sautéed chestnuts, to serve

Trim the beef and rub the pepper into the surface. Place on a tray and leave in the fridge uncovered overnight.

Preheat the oven to 400°F. Place the garlic bulbs on a baking sheet. Bake for 30 minutes, then remove and allow to cool. Slice the bulbs in half and squeeze out the garlic cloves. Mash them into the butter, then mix in the horseradish and season.

Place the beef into a roasting pan and roast for 10 minutes. Remove the beef from the oven, turn it over, and roast for an additional 5 minutes.

Season the beef with salt, cover with foil, and allow to rest for 15 minutes. Drain any juices from the roasting pan, reserving them for later.

Return the beef to the oven for an additional 10–15 minutes, depending on how rare you like your beef. Serve in thick slices with the garlic butter, a drizzle of the pan juices, and some sautéed baby carrots and chestnuts. Season with black pepper.

ginger-spiced pork chops

serves 4

1 teaspoon smoked paprika
1 teaspoon garam masala
1/2 teaspoon ground turmeric
1 tablespoon soft brown sugar
11/2 tablespoons grated fresh ginger
2 garlic cloves, crushed
4 tablespoons olive oil
4 pork chops
mashed potatoes (see basics), to serve
green salad and lemon wedges,
   to serve

Put the paprika, garam masala, turmeric, sugar, ginger, and garlic into a bowl. Stir in the olive oil to make a thick paste. Cover the pork chops with the paste and allow to marinate for 30 minutes.

Heat a large nonstick frying pan over high heat and sear the pork chops for 3 minutes. Turn the chops over, reduce the heat to low, and cook for an additional 7–10 minutes, depending on the thickness. If the chops are thick, cover the pan with a lid. Serve with mashed potatoes, green salad, and a wedge of lemon.

lime and coconut fish

2 garlic cloves

1¼-inch piece galangal, peeled and
  chopped

3 small red chilies, seeded and
  chopped

1¼-inch piece ginger, peeled and
  chopped

2 lemongrass stems, trimmed and
  chopped

15 macadamia nuts

2 tablespoons olive oil

2 red onions, peeled and finely sliced

8 Kaffir lime leaves

14-ounce can coconut milk

2 tomatoes, diced

1¼ pounds firm whitefish fillets, cut
  into large chunks

sea salt and freshly ground black
  pepper, to season

cilantro sprigs, to garnish

steamed rice, to serve

Put the garlic, galangal, chilies, ginger, lemongrass, and macadamia nuts into a food processor or blender and process until a thick paste forms.

Heat the olive oil in a frying pan over medium heat and add the onions and lime leaves. Cook until the onions are soft.

Add the spice paste and stir until aromatic. Add the coconut milk, tomatoes, and fish, then simmer for 8 minutes. Season to taste with sea salt and freshly ground black pepper. Garnish with cilantro sprigs and serve with steamed rice.

spiced lentils with lamb chops

serves 4

2 tablespoons olive oil
2 garlic cloves, crushed
1 red onion, finely diced
1 teaspoon finely chopped canned
   chipotle chili
1 teaspoon ground turmeric
1/2 cup Puy lentils
13/4 cups canned tomatoes, roughly
   chopped
sea salt and pepper, to season
12 small French-trimmed lamb chops
1 handful cilantro leaves

Put the olive oil in a saucepan over medium heat. Add the garlic, onion, chili, and turmeric, and cook until the onion is soft and transparent. Add the lentils and cook for 1 minute, stirring the lentils into the onion mixture. Add the tomato and 2 cups water. Cover with a lid and allow to simmer for 40 minutes. When the lentils are cooked, remove from the heat and season to taste.

In a nonstick frying pan over high heat, sear the lamb chops on one side. Cook until the uncooked side begins to look a little bloody, then turn the chops over and cook for an additional 1–2 minutes. Season with sea salt and allow to rest for a few minutes.

Spoon the lentils onto four warmed plates. Top with the chops and garnish with cilantro leaves.

fish with a creamy
saffron sauce

serves 4

12 saffron threads

1 tablespoon olive oil

6 red Asian shallots, finely diced

1 large red chili, seeded and finely
chopped

1 teaspoon yellow mustard seeds

1 tomato, diced

1 teaspoon soft brown sugar

four 6-ounce perch fillets

4 handfuls baby spinach leaves

3/4 cup coconut milk

lime halves and steamed white rice,
to serve

Cover the saffron with 1 cup boiling water in a small bowl. Heat a large deep frying pan over medium heat and add the olive oil and shallots. When the shallots are soft and transparent, add the chili, mustard seeds, tomato, sugar, and saffron water. Simmer for 3 minutes before adding the fish fillets. Cover and cook for 5 minutes.

Place the fish fillets on four serving plates and pile the spinach leaves beside them. Add the coconut milk to the sauce and simmer for 1 minute before spooning over the fish. Serve with lime and steamed white rice.

spiced duck breast   serves 4

4 duck breast fillets, skin on
2 tablespoons soft brown sugar
1/2 teaspoon Szechuan peppercorns
1 star anise
1 tablespoon sea salt
1/2 cup brandy
4 dried shiitake mushrooms
2 thin leeks, cut into 3/4-inch lengths
2²/3 cups cubed squash
2 tablespoons light olive oil

Preheat the oven to 350°F. Score the skin of the duck in a crisscross pattern. Put the sugar, peppercorns, and star anise into a mortar and pestle with the sea salt and grind together. Rub this mixture into the duck skin. Put the brandy in a shallow dish, add the duck breasts, skin side up, then cover and marinate for at least 1 hour or overnight.

Soak the dried mushrooms in 2 cups boiling water for 30 minutes. Strain the liquid into a baking dish. Slice the mushrooms and put them in the baking dish with the leeks and squash. Season, cover with foil, and bake for 30 minutes or until the squash is soft. Increase the oven temperature to 400°F.

Heat the oil in a frying pan over high heat. Sear the duck, skin side down, until lightly browned. Put the duck breasts on a rack set over a baking sheet, skin side up. Drizzle with the brandy marinade and roast for about 15 minutes. Arrange the squash and leeks on four plates. Top with thinly sliced duck breast.

spiced ocean trout   serves 4

2 tablespoons cumin seeds
1 tablespoon coriander seeds
2 tablespoons olive oil
2 leeks, washed and finely sliced
2 carrots, peeled and finely sliced
2 celery stalks, finely sliced
1 cup white wine
four 6 1/2-ounce ocean trout fillets
sea salt and freshly ground black
 pepper, to season
1 lemon, juiced
mashed potatoes (see basics), to serve

Put the cumin and coriander seeds in a large heavy-based frying pan over medium heat. Heat until the seeds are aromatic. Remove from the frying pan and grind in a blender or a mortar and pestle.

Return the spices to the frying pan and add the olive oil and leeks. Cook over medium heat for 5 minutes. Add the carrots and celery, and cook for an additional few minutes, until both begin to soften.

Add the wine and 1/2 cup water, and place the trout fillets over this mixture. Season with sea salt and freshly ground black pepper. Cover the pan with a lid and reduce the heat to a simmer. Cook for 6 minutes. Remove from the heat and drizzle the lemon juice over the fish fillets.

Serve with mashed potatoes and a spoonful of the spicy sauce.

peppered beef with mashed winter squash serves 6

3 1/4-pound beef tenderloin
2 tablespoons freshly ground
  black pepper
sea salt, to season
1 winter squash (about 2 1/4 pounds)
2/3 cup butter
2 garlic cloves, crushed
1/2 cup finely chopped chives

Trim the beef, then rub the pepper into the surface. Place on a tray and refrigerate uncovered overnight.

Preheat the oven to 400°F. Place the beef in a roasting pan and roast for 10 minutes, then turn and cook for an additional 5 minutes. Remove from the oven and season with sea salt. Cover with foil and allow to rest for 15 minutes. Drain any juices from the pan and reserve.

Peel and cut the winter squash into small pieces. Place it in a saucepan with salted cold water and bring to a boil. Cook until tender.

Melt the butter in a small saucepan over medium heat. Add the garlic and chives, then simmer for a few minutes. When the squash is cooked, drain and mash. Stir in the butter mixture and whip until fluffy. Cover and set aside in a warm place.

Return the beef to the oven for an additional 15 minutes. Serve in thick slices with a drizzle of pan juices and a large spoonful of the mashed squash.

snapper fillets with a pink peppercorn dressing

serves 4

4 tablespoons olive oil
2 tablespoons lime juice
1 teaspoon pink peppercorns
1 tablespoon finely chopped pickled
    ginger
1 handful cilantro leaves
1 tablespoon finely chopped
    lemongrass
four 7-ounce snapper fillets, skin on
sea salt, to season
2 tablespoons vegetable oil
steamed green beans, sliced
    diagonally, to serve

To make the dressing, put the olive oil, lime juice, peppercorns, pickled ginger, cilantro, and lemongrass in a bowl and stir to combine.

Rinse the snapper fillets under cold running water and pat dry with paper towels. Season both sides of the fillets with sea salt.

Heat the vegetable oil in a frying pan over high heat and add the snapper, skin side down. Using a spatula, press the surface of the fish and cook for 1 minute, or until the skin is crispy. Turn the fillets over, reduce the heat to medium, and cook for 8 minutes.

Spoon the pink peppercorn dressing over the snapper and serve with steamed green beans.

chicken in a smoked chili marinade

serves 4

1 tablespoon finely chopped canned
  chipotle chili
1 teaspoon dried oregano
2 tablespoons tomato paste
2 tablespoons molasses or light corn
  syrup
1 orange, zested and juiced
4 chicken leg quarters
green salad and minted yogurt,
  to serve

Preheat the oven to 400°F. Put the chili, oregano, tomato paste, molasses, orange zest, and orange juice in a large bowl and stir to combine. Add the chicken pieces and toss to coat. Cover and allow to marinate for at least 1 hour.

Place the chicken pieces on a baking sheet and roast for 35–40 minutes. Insert a sharp knife into the thickest part of the chicken and ensure that the juices are clear. Serve with a green salad and minted yogurt.

velvet salt pork with wild mushrooms

serves 4

1³/4 pounds salt pork
1 cup soy sauce
2 cups chicken stock (see basics)
1¹/2 teaspoons Chinese five-spice
2 red chilies
1 cinnamon stick
4 star anise
1 tablespoon finely grated ginger
2 garlic cloves, crushed
1 tablespoon grated jaggery (or brown sugar)
12 fresh shiitake mushrooms
2 tablespoons vegetable oil
1¹/2 cups oyster mushrooms
1¹/2 cups enoki mushrooms
steamed white rice, to serve

Preheat the oven to 350°F. Put the pork in a saucepan and cover with water. Bring to a boil, then remove, drain, and rinse.

Put the soy sauce, stock, ¹/2 teaspoon of the five-spice, the chilies, cinnamon stick, star anise, ginger, and garlic in a baking dish. Add the pork, skin side up, and rub the skin with the remaining five-spice. Add enough water to cover most of the pork. Cover with foil and bake for 4 hours.

Remove the pork from the baking dish. Place onto a baking sheet. Cover and refrigerate overnight. Reserve 1¹/2 cups of the cooking liquid.

Slice the pork into 3¹/4 x 1¹/4-inch strips. Put the reserved cooking liquid into a saucepan with the jaggery and shiitake mushrooms. Bring to a boil. Reduce the heat and simmer for 10 minutes.

Heat the oil in a large nonstick frying pan and fry the salt pork until crisp. Add the oyster and enoki mushrooms to the saucepan just before serving. Serve with steamed white rice.

spiced kumquat chicken

serves 4

1 whole 4-pound chicken
16 fresh kumquats, halved
4 star anise
1 teaspoon Szechuan peppercorns
3 tablespoons dessert wine, optional
2 tablespoons tamari or light soy sauce
mashed potatoes (see basics) and
   steamed green beans, to serve

Preheat the oven to 400°F. Rinse the chicken and pat dry with paper towels. Put the kumquats, star anise, peppercorns, and dessert wine in a small bowl and toss to combine. Put the spiced kumquats into the cavity of the chicken. Using a skewer, secure the opening so that the kumquats remain within the chicken.

Rub the skin of the chicken with the tamari and bake for 1 hour 15 minutes, or until cooked through. Remove the chicken and check that it is cooked by pulling a leg away from the body—the juices should be clear and not pink.

Allow the chicken to rest for 10 minutes before carving. Serve with a spoonful of the baked kumquats, mashed potatoes, and steamed green beans.

cinnamon french toast rosewater fruit salad banana and berry muffins peach waffles papaya and coconut sambal sticky black rice hazelnut meringue with berries cinnamon jam drops cinnamon quince with orange mascarpone apple and blackberry cobbler berry chocolate tart peach and blueberry shortcake rhubarb fool chili and vanilla syrup with fresh mango blood plum and cinnamon jellies eccles cakes tamarind

04   sweets

ginger ice cream with red papaya ice-cream trifles with turkish delight cumin and lime cookies jaffa mousse spiced syrup tarts frozen raspberry whip with strawberries rhubarb syllabub spiced yogurt with fresh fruit rhubarb gelatin bitter chocolate tartlet

cinnamon french toast

serves 5

5 thick slices white bread,
  crusts removed
1 egg
1 tablespoon sugar
1 teaspoon ground cinnamon
1/2 cup milk
butter, for pan-frying
extra sugar, for sprinkling
2/3 cup plain yogurt, to serve
fresh seasonal fruit, to serve
1/3 cup maple syrup, to serve
2 tablespoons finely chopped
  toasted pecans, to serve

Cut each slice of bread in half to make rectangles. Beat the egg, sugar, and cinnamon in a bowl, then add the milk. Melt some butter in a frying pan over medium heat. Dip the bread into the milk mixture, covering both sides. Sprinkle one side of each piece of bread with sugar and gently fry, sugar side down, for 3 minutes or until golden. Sprinkle the tops with a little more sugar and flip over. Cook until golden and serve with yogurt, fruit, maple syrup, and a sprinkle of pecans.

rosewater fruit salad serves 6

1/2 cup dried figs
1/2 cup dried apricots
1/3 cup pitted prunes
1/4 cup sugar
3 tablespoons orange juice
1 cinnamon stick
2 star anise
1/2 teaspoon rosewater
1 cup plain yogurt, to serve
1 cup flaked toasted almonds, to serve

Cut the dried fruit into bite-sized pieces and place in a small bowl. Put the sugar, 1 cup of water, the orange juice, cinnamon stick, and star anise in a small saucepan. Bring to a boil over medium heat, stirring to dissolve the sugar. Boil gently for 5–6 minutes until a light syrup forms. Remove from the heat and stir in the rosewater.

Pour the liquid over the prepared dried fruit and allow to soak for several hours or preferably overnight.

Serve with yogurt, sprinkled with the flaked almonds.

banana and berry muffins

2 cups all-purpose flour
2 teaspoons baking powder
1/2 teaspoon ground cinnamon
pinch salt
2 ripe bananas, mashed
1 cup fresh or frozen blueberries
3 tablespoons honey
3 tablespoons vegetable oil
1 large egg
3/4 cup milk
4 strawberries, halved
cinnamon sugar, for sprinkling

Preheat the oven to 350°F. Sift the flour, baking powder, cinnamon, and the pinch of salt into a large bowl. Add the bananas and blueberries and, using a fork, lightly toss the fruit through the flour. Whisk together the honey, vegetable oil, egg, and milk in a small bowl. Add the liquid ingredients to the dry ingredients and combine.

Spoon the batter into a lightly greased 8-hole muffin pan. Top each with a strawberry half and sprinkle with cinnamon sugar. Bake for 20 minutes and serve immediately.

peach waffles

waffles

2 cups self-rising flour

2 teaspoons ground cinnamon

3/4 cup superfine sugar

1/3 cup butter, melted

3 eggs, separated

21/2 cups milk

1/2 cup sugar

1/2 vanilla bean, split and seeds scraped

juice of 1 lemon

2 large freestone peaches, peeled, pitted, and cut into eighths

To make the waffles, sift the flour and cinnamon into a bowl. Add the sugar, mix well, and make a well in the center. In a jug, mix together the melted butter, egg yolks, and milk, and pour quickly into the flour mixture, whisking to form a smooth batter.

In a separate bowl, whisk the egg whites until soft peaks form and gently fold through the batter.

Preheat and lightly grease a waffle iron. Spoon a small amount of the batter onto the iron, close the lid, and cook the waffle until golden. Repeat with the remaining batter.

Put 12/3 cups water, the sugar, vanilla seeds, and the lemon juice in a saucepan and bring to a boil, stirring to dissolve the sugar. Add the peaches and return to a boil. Reduce the heat and simmer gently for 2 minutes. Place the fruit in a bowl and reduce the liquid over medium heat for 10–15 minutes to produce a thick syrup. Pour over the peaches. Serve waffles topped with a piece of peach and drizzle with the syrup.

sticky black rice   serves 4

1 cup black rice
1/3 cup soft brown sugar
pinch salt
1/2 cup coconut milk
red papaya or banana, to serve

Soak the black rice in plenty of cold water for 1 hour. Drain, then rinse. Drain again and put into a saucepan with 2 cups water. Bring to a boil, stirring occasionally, then reduce the heat to low, cover, and allow to simmer for 35 minutes.

Remove the lid and stir in the sugar, the pinch of salt, and the coconut milk. Simmer over low heat for an additional 10 minutes, then remove and allow to cool. Serve spooned over sliced red papaya or banana and drizzle with extra coconut milk.

hazelnut meringue with berries

serves 6

2 egg whites
1/2 cup superfine sugar
1/3 cup ground hazelnuts
1 1/4 cups light whipping cream
1 teaspoon natural vanilla extract
3 cups mixed strawberries (quartered),
   raspberries, and blackberries

Preheat the oven to 300°F. Whisk the egg whites until they form soft peaks and then slowly add the sugar, continuing to beat until the mixture stiffens. Fold in the hazelnuts.

Line two baking sheets with parchment paper. Divide the meringue mixture between them, putting a big dollop in the middle of each sheet. Using the back of a spoon, spread the mixture out until you have two 8-inch circles.

Bake for 40 minutes. Turn the oven off, but leave the meringues in the oven for 30 minutes with the door ajar.

Whip the cream and fold in the vanilla extract. When the meringues are cool, put one of the rounds on a serving plate and top with some of the cream and half the berries, arranging them so that they make a flat surface for the next meringue layer. Put the other meringue on top and decorate with the cream and remaining berries. Allow to sit for 15 minutes before serving.

cinnamon jam drops　　makes 36

3/4 cup self-rising flour
1 teaspoon ground cinnamon
1/4 cup rice flour
1/3 cup unsalted butter, softened
1/3 cup sugar
1 egg, beaten
1 1/2 cups berry jam

Preheat the oven to 350°F. Sift together the flour, cinnamon, and rice flour. In a bowl, cream the butter and sugar until light and fluffy, then gradually add the egg, beating well. Fold into the sifted ingredients until just combined.

Roll a teaspoon of the batter into a ball and place on a baking sheet lined with parchment paper. Repeat with the remaining mixture. Press a deep indent into the center of each ball and fill with a little berry jam. Bake for 8–10 minutes, or until golden.

cinnamon quince with orange mascarpone

serves 4

3 quinces

3/4 cup red wine

1/2 cup fresh orange juice

1/3 cup soft brown sugar

1 cinnamon stick

orange mascarpone (see basics), to
  serve

gingerbread (see basics), to serve

Preheat the oven to 350°F. Peel and core the quinces, slice into eighths, and put in a baking dish. Mix together the wine, orange juice, and sugar, and pour the mixture over the quince pieces. Add the cinnamon stick and 1 cup water, cover with foil, and bake for 2 hours.

Remove the foil and turn the quince pieces to coat in the liquid. Bake for an additional hour, or until the liquid has reduced to a syrup.

Divide the quinces between four plates and serve with a dollop of orange mascarpone and a drizzle of the quince syrup. For a richer wintertime dessert, serve the quince with slices of gingerbread.

apple and blackberry cobbler

serves 6

2 cups all-purpose flour

1 tablespoon baking powder

3/4 cup superfine sugar

pinch salt

1/4 cup vegetable shortening

3 1/2 tablespoons unsalted butter

1 egg

4 tablespoons milk

6 green apples, peeled, cored, and cut into eighths

2 1/3 cups frozen blackberries

2 tablespoons lemon juice

1 teaspoon cinnamon

whipped cream, to serve

Preheat the oven to 415°F. Combine the flour, baking powder, 1 tablespoon of the sugar, and the pinch of salt in a large bowl. Cut the shortening and butter into small cubes and rub into the flour with your fingertips until the mixture resembles bread crumbs.

Whisk together the egg and milk, then stir into the flour mixture until combined. Turn the dough out onto a floured surface and knead.

Combine the apples, blackberries, 4 tablespoons of the sugar, lemon juice, and cinnamon, and put in a deep baking dish. Break off pieces of the dough and scatter them over the top of the fruit until roughly covered. Sprinkle with the remaining sugar and bake for 40 minutes. Serve with whipped cream.

berry chocolate tart serves 8

1/3 cup strawberry jam
1 prebaked chocolate tart shell
 (see basics)
2/3 cup unsalted butter
11/3 cups chopped dark chocolate
3 egg yolks
2 eggs
1/3 cup superfine sugar
2 tablespoons Grand Marnier
unsweetened cocoa powder,
 for dusting
fresh berries, to serve

Preheat the oven to 350°F. Spoon the jam over the base of the tart shell and bake for 2 minutes. Remove the tart shell from the oven and use a pastry brush to spread the warm jam gently over the base until it is glazed all over.

Melt the butter and chocolate together in a saucepan over low heat. Beat the yolks, eggs, and sugar until they are fluffy. Pour the melted chocolate and Grand Marnier into the eggs and continue to beat for 1 minute.

Pour the chocolate filling into the tart shell and return to the oven for 5 minutes. Allow to sit for at least 2 hours before serving. Dust with cocoa powder and serve with fresh berries.

peach and blueberry shortcake

1/2 cup all-purpose flour

1/4 cup cornstarch

1/4 cup soft brown sugar

1/2 teaspoon ground ginger

1/2 teaspoon baking powder

1 1/2 tablespoons unsalted butter, softened

1 egg yolk

1 cup blueberries

3 tablespoons superfine sugar

2 peaches, peeled, pitted, and sliced

confectioners' sugar, for dusting

whipped cream, to serve

Preheat the oven to 350°F. Sift the flour, cornstarch, brown sugar, ginger, and baking powder into a bowl, then work in the butter and the egg yolk to form a soft dough. If the dough is too stiff, add a splash of cold water. Roll out the pastry and cut into four 3-inch rounds.

Put the rounds on a baking sheet lined with parchment paper. Bake for 12 minutes or until golden brown. Allow to cool.

In a nonstick frying pan over medium heat, add 2 tablespoons water, the blueberries, and the superfine sugar. Heat until the sugar melts and the berries look glossy and their skins start to split. Arrange the shortcakes on four plates with the peaches on top. Spoon the berries over the top and dust with confectioners' sugar. Serve with whipped cream.

rhubarb fool

serves 4

7–8 stems rhubarb (about 14 ounces)
2 tablespoons sugar
2 oranges, juiced
1/2 cup dark brown sugar
1 1/4 cups light whipping cream,
  whipped
cardamom almond bread (see basics),
  to serve

Trim and rinse the rhubarb before chopping into 3/4-inch lengths. Put the rhubarb into a saucepan over low heat with the sugar and orange juice. Cover and simmer for 15 minutes. Remove from the heat and allow to cool.

Spoon a little of the rhubarb into the base of four glass serving bowls. Sprinkle with the brown sugar and top with the whipped cream. Spoon another layer of rhubarb over the cream and lightly sprinkle with more brown sugar. Serve with cardamom almond bread.

chili and vanilla syrup
with fresh mango   serves 4

1 cup sugar
1 vanilla bean, split lengthwise
1 large red chili, seeded and finely
   chopped
1 lime, juiced
3 mangoes, peeled and flesh cut into
   thick strips
lime sorbet (see basics), to serve

Put the sugar, vanilla bean, and chili into a small saucepan with 2 cups water. Bring to a boil, then reduce the heat and allow to simmer for 15 minutes. Allow to cool, then stir in the lime juice and strain.

Divide the mangoes between four chilled bowls and top with scoops of lime sorbet. Drizzle with the chili syrup and serve immediately.

blood plum and cinnamon jellies

6 blood plums, quartered and pitted
1 cup superfine sugar
1 cinnamon stick
1 vanilla bean, split in half lengthwise
1–2 oranges, juiced
1 ounce powdered gelatin
light whipping cream, to serve

Put the plums, sugar, cinnamon stick, vanilla bean, and 3 cups water into a saucepan. Bring to a boil, then reduce the heat. Continue to simmer for 30 minutes. Remove from the heat and strain the plum syrup through a fine sieve or muslin. Pour the syrup into a large measuring jug and add enough orange juice to make 2 cups of plum syrup.

Dissolve the gelatin in 1/2 cup hot water, then stir into the plum syrup. Stir well for a couple of minutes to ensure that the gelatin is thoroughly mixed into the liquid.

Pour the gelatin into six 1/2-cup molds and refrigerate for 3 hours, or until set. Serve with a drizzle of cream.

citrus syrup cake   serves 10

1 cup unsalted butter
1 heaping cup superfine sugar
4 eggs
scant 1/2 cup plain yogurt
2 lemons, zested and juiced
2 oranges, zested and juiced
2 limes, zested and juiced
2 cups self-rising flour
1 cup sugar
whipped cream, to serve

Preheat the oven to 350°F. Grease and line a 9 1/2-inch springform pan with parchment paper. Cream the butter and sugar, then fold in the eggs, yogurt, and citrus zest. Sift in the flour and fold it through the batter. Spoon the batter into the prepared pan. Bake for 45 minutes, or until the cake is golden brown and a skewer inserted into the center comes out clean.

Meanwhile, put the citrus juice in a saucepan and add the sugar. Bring to a boil and stir until the sugar dissolves. Remove from the heat.

When the cake is cooked, remove from the oven and prick the top of the cake all over with a skewer. Pour half the syrup over the top, reserving the rest for serving. Allow to cool.

Slice and serve with the reserved syrup and whipped cream.

tamarind ginger ice cream
with red papaya

serves 4

4 egg yolks
2/3 cup superfine sugar
1 cup milk
1/3 cup tamarind puree
1 1/4 cups light whipping cream
1/2 cup finely sliced ginger in syrup
2 small ripe red papayas, halved,
seeded, and peeled

Whisk the yolks with the sugar in a bowl until doubled in volume. Bring the milk to a boil in a saucepan and, when it begins to froth, pour it into the yolk mixture. Whisk together before returning to the saucepan and placing over low heat. Stir until the mixture thickens and coats the back of a wooden spoon. Remove from the heat and strain into a chilled bowl. Stir in the tamarind puree, cream, and ginger. Allow to cool.

Pour the mixture into an ice-cream machine. Churn according to the manufacturer's instructions.

If you don't have an ice-cream machine, pour the mixture into a small metal bowl and place in the freezer. Take the ice cream mixture out of the freezer every couple of hours and beat. This will break up any ice crystals as they form. Serve the ice cream scooped into a red papaya half.

ice-cream trifles
with turkish delight serves 6

2¹/2 cups raspberries or
  2 cups strawberries
6 cubes Turkish delight
12 plain chocolate cookies
2 cups vanilla ice cream (see basics),
  scooped
1/2 cup blanched almonds, toasted

Puree the berries to form a sauce and set aside. Cut the Turkish delight into eighths to make small cubes. Break the cookies into small pieces and set aside.

Layer the ice cream, cookies, Turkish delight, and almonds into six chilled glasses and top with the berry sauce. Serve immediately.

cumin and lime cookies

1/2 cup unsalted butter
2/3 cup superfine sugar
1 teaspoon ground cumin
1 teaspoon natural vanilla extract
2 tablespoons lime juice, plus the
   grated zest of 1 lime
1 egg
11/4 cups all-purpose flour
1 teaspoon baking powder
whipped cream and fresh fruit, to serve

Preheat the oven to 350°F. Cream the butter and sugar, then fold in the cumin, vanilla, lime juice, lime zest, and egg. Sift in the flour and baking powder and stir together. Spoon the batter onto a baking sheet lined with parchment paper—use 1 heaping tablespoon of mixture per cookie. Bake for 12 minutes or until golden brown. Allow to cool on a wire rack.

Serve with whipped cream and slices of ripe fruit such as figs, nectarines, and peaches.

jaffa mousse

1 cup chopped bitter chocolate
4 tablespoons Grand Marnier
4 egg yolks
1/3 cup unsweetened cocoa powder
2 teaspoons grated orange zest
3/4 cup light whipping cream, whipped
4 oranges

Melt the chocolate and 2 tablespoons of the Grand Marnier in a bowl set over a saucepan of simmering water. Add the egg yolks, one at a time, stirring each one well into the chocolate mixture before adding the next. The chocolate may begin to stiffen, but it will soon become smooth again. When you have added all the yolks, remove the chocolate mixture from the heat and allow to cool slightly.

Fold the cocoa and grated orange zest into the whipped cream, then fold the cream into the chocolate. Pour the mixture into a bowl and refrigerate for several hours to chill.

Peel the oranges with a sharp knife and cut into slices. Put the orange slices in a bowl with the remaining Grand Marnier. Divide the oranges between dessert plates and top with a spoonful of the mousse.

spiced syrup tarts   makes 24

1/2 cup dried coconut

1/2 cup light corn syrup or maple syrup

1/4 teaspoon ground cardamom

1 tablespoon lime juice

2 teaspoons finely chopped lime zest

1 egg yolk, beaten

24 prebaked sweet tartlet shells
  (see basics)

confectioners' sugar, for dusting

Preheat the oven to 350°F. Put the coconut, syrup, cardamom, lime juice, lime zest, and beaten egg yolk in a bowl and mix. Spoon a heaping teaspoon into each pastry shell and bake for 10 minutes. Remove and cool on a wire rack. Dust with confectioners' sugar before serving.

frozen raspberry whip with strawberries

serves 4-6

1 1/2 cups raspberries
1 teaspoon lemon juice
1/2 cup superfine sugar
1 egg white
4 cups strawberries
1 tablespoon confectioners' sugar

Whip the raspberries, lemon juice, sugar, and egg white with electric beaters for 10 minutes, or until the mixture is light and fluffy and has tripled in size. Spoon into a container and freeze for several hours or overnight until frozen.

Just prior to serving, hull and halve the strawberries, reserving a few whole ones. Sprinkle the strawberry halves with the confectioners' sugar and lightly toss until well coated. Set aside for 5 minutes before serving with a scoop of the frozen raspberry whip. Garnish with the whole strawberries.

rhubarb syllabub

serves 8

10 stems rhubarb (about 18 ounces),
  cut into small pieces
1/3 cup superfine sugar
1 cup light whipping cream
16 macaroons or amaretti
4 tablespoons Madeira
1 teaspoon finely grated lemon zest
1/4 teaspoon almond extract

Put the rhubarb in a saucepan with the sugar, then cover and cook over medium heat until the rhubarb is soft, stirring occasionally to prevent it from sticking. Allow to cool.

Whip the cream. Refrigerate and cover until needed.

Crumble two macaroons into each of eight glasses. Fold the Madeira, lemon zest, and almond extract into the rhubarb before lightly folding the rhubarb through the whipped cream. Spoon the rhubarb cream over the macaroons and serve.

spiced yogurt
with fresh fruit

serves 6

2 cinnamon sticks
2 star anise
2 cloves
2 vanilla beans, split lengthwise
2 cardamom pods, split
1 cup light whipping cream
1 tablespoon sugar
1 1/4 cups Greek-style yogurt
fresh fruit, to serve

Put the cinnamon sticks, star anise, cloves, vanilla beans, cardamom pods, and cream in a small saucepan over low heat. Allow to simmer for 30 minutes. Remove from the heat, strain, then stir in the sugar before allowing to cool.

Fold the spiced cream through the yogurt and serve drizzled over fruit.

rhubarb gelatin   serves 8

2¹/₄ pounds rhubarb (about 20 stems)
1¹/₂ cups superfine sugar
grated zest and juice of 1 orange
1 teaspoon ground cinnamon
1¹/₄ cups additional orange juice
1¹/₂ ounces powdered gelatin
vanilla ice cream (see basics), to serve

Preheat the oven to 350°F. Chop the rhubarb into 1¹/₄-inch lengths and put in a ovenproof glass or ceramic dish. Add the sugar, orange zest and juice, cinnamon, and 2 cups water. Cover with foil. Bake for 1 hour. Strain the rhubarb through a sieve into a jug. Add enough additional orange juice to make up to 3 cups of liquid.

Lightly oil a jelly mold or glass bowl with vegetable oil, then set aside.

Dissolve the gelatin in ¹/₂ cup hot water, then stir into the warm rhubarb syrup. Stir well for a couple of minutes to ensure the gelatin is thoroughly mixed with the liquid.

Pour the gelatin into the mold. Refrigerate for 5 hours to chill and set.

To turn out, warm the outside of the mold with a cloth rinsed in hot water, cover with a plate, then turn it over. Serve with vanilla ice cream.

bitter chocolate tartlets

serves 6

2/3 cup unsalted butter

1/3 cup chopped dark chocolate

3 egg yolks

2 eggs

1/4 cup superfine sugar

2 tablespoons Tia Maria

6 prebaked mini short-crust tartlet
  shells (see basics)

unsweetened cocoa powder,
  for dusting

whipped cream, to serve

Preheat the oven to 350°F. Melt the butter and chocolate together in a saucepan over very low heat. Beat the egg yolks, eggs, and sugar until light and fluffy. Pour the melted chocolate and Tia Maria into the egg mixture and continue to beat for 1 minute. Pour the chocolate filling into the tart shells and bake for 5 minutes.

Remove from the oven and allow to sit for 1 hour before serving. Dust with cocoa powder and serve with whipped cream.

coffee granita

1/2 cup sugar
1 teaspoon finely grated lemon zest
1 tablespoon lemon juice
2 cups strong espresso

Put the sugar and 1/2 cup water in a saucepan over high heat. Stir until the sugar has dissolved. Remove from the heat and stir in the lemon zest, lemon juice, and coffee. Allow to cool, then cover and chill in the refrigerator.

Pour the chilled mixture into a cake pan or large shallow metal container. (The mixture must freeze quickly, and a shallow metal container chills the liquid faster.) Cover and put in the freezer. After 1 hour, use a fork to drag the icy crystals from the edges of the container into the center. Return to the freezer and repeat this process every 30 minutes, until the mixture is completely frozen and icy.

If making in advance, remove from the freezer 1 hour before serving, thaw slightly, then break up the crystals again and return to the freezer for an additional 30 minutes before serving.

blackberry fool

serves 4

2¹/₂ cups blackberries
¹/₄ cup superfine sugar
2 tablespoons crème de framboise
  (optional)
1 teaspoon orange-flower water
1¹/₄ cups light whipping cream,
  whipped
almond bread or biscotti, to serve

Put the blackberries, sugar, liqueur, and orange-flower water into a blender or food processor and blend to a puree.

Fold the pureed berries into the cream and spoon the mixture into four chilled glasses or small bowls. Serve with almond bread or biscotti.

ginger hearts

2 cups all-purpose flour
1 teaspoon baking powder
3 teaspoons ground ginger
1 teaspoon ground cinnamon
pinch of ground cloves
1/3 cup unsalted butter, softened
1/2 cup dark brown sugar
1 egg
1 tablespoon molasses
1/4 cup raw or demerara sugar

Preheat the oven to 350°F. Sift the flour and spices into a bowl. In another bowl, cream the butter and brown sugar until light and fluffy, then add the egg, beating well. Stir the molasses through the butter mixture, then fold through the sifted dry ingredients until combined. Gather into a ball.

Roll out the dough between two sheets of parchment paper to a thickness of 1/4 inch. Cut heart shapes from the dough with a 2-inch cookie cutter and sprinkle with raw sugar. Transfer to a baking sheet and bake for 12 minutes. Cool on a wire rack.

berry granita

3/4 cup superfine sugar
21/2 cups hot Earl Grey tea
2 cups strawberries
juice of 1 orange
11/2 cups raspberries, to serve

Dissolve the sugar in the hot tea and set aside to cool. In a blender or food processor, blend the strawberries with the orange juice to a puree. Stir the pureed strawberries into the cool tea and pour into a plastic container measuring about 6 x 8 inches. Cover and put in the freezer for 2 hours.

Remove from the freezer and use a fork to break up the ice crystals, mixing them back into the chilled liquid. Repeat this process every 40 minutes until you have a container filled with flavored crushed ice.

If freezing overnight, remove from the freezer and allow it to soften for 30 minutes before breaking up the crystals and returning to the freezer.

To serve, layer the granita with the raspberries in tall glasses.

baked quinces with orange and cardamom almond bread

serves 4

2 large quinces, peeled, cored, and
  quartered
2 oranges, juiced
1/4 cup sugar
2 tablespoons honey
cardamom almond bread (see basics)
confectioners' sugar, for dusting
plain yogurt or heavy cream, to serve

Preheat the oven to 350°F. Line a baking sheet with parchment paper and lay the quince quarters on it. Cover them with the orange juice, sugar, honey, and another piece of parchment paper. Bake for 1 hour.

Reduce the oven temperature to 275°F and bake the quinces for an additional 2 hours, or until they are soft and have turned a deep ruby red.

Serve the quinces with cardamom almond bread dusted with a little confectioners' sugar, and with yogurt or heavy cream.

sticky date pudding

scant 1 cup pitted and finely chopped
  dates
1$\frac{1}{2}$ teaspoons baking soda
3$\frac{1}{2}$ tablespoons unsalted butter
$\frac{2}{3}$ cup soft brown sugar
2 eggs
1 teaspoon natural vanilla extract
1 tablespoon finely chopped
  crystallized ginger
1 cup sifted self-rising flour
butterscotch sauce and whipped
  cream, to serve

Preheat the oven to 350°F. Lightly grease four 1$\frac{1}{4}$-cup ramekins. Place the dates in a bowl with the baking soda. Pour over a scant $\frac{2}{3}$ cup boiling water and set aside for 10 minutes.

Beat the butter with the sugar in a bowl until pale and creamy. Whisk in the eggs. Stir in the vanilla extract and add the crystallized ginger. Add the flour and lightly fold it through the batter. Fold the date mixture through.

Spoon the batter into the ramekins and put the ramekins onto a baking sheet. Bake for 20–25 minutes, or until firm. Serve with butterscotch sauce and whipped cream.

rose-tinged rice pudding

serves 6

2 cups milk

1/4 cup sugar

2 teaspoons finely grated orange zest

pinch salt

1/3 cup short-grained rice

1/2 cup light whipping cream, whipped

1 teaspoon rosewater

11/2 cups raspberries

1/2 cup raw pistachio kernels, chopped

Bring the milk to a boil in a saucepan with the sugar, orange zest, and the pinch of salt. Add the rice, reduce the heat, and simmer for 30 minutes, stirring occasionally. When the rice has cooked, allow it to cool before folding in the whipped cream and rosewater.

Spoon the rice pudding into serving bowls and top with the raspberries and pistachios.

nectarine salad

8 nectarines, pitted and sliced into
   eighths
1 1/2 cups raspberries
1 tablespoon grated fresh ginger
1/4 cup soft brown sugar
1 lime, juiced
plain yogurt, to serve

Put all the ingredients except the yogurt in a large bowl and gently toss together. Allow the salad to marinate for 1 hour. Serve with plain yogurt.

chocolate parfait

heaping 1/2 cup sugar

heaping 3/4 cup chopped dark
   chocolate, broken into pieces

4 egg yolks

1 1/4 cups light whipping cream,
   whipped

1 tablespoon Frangelico

1/2 cup toasted flaked almonds

fresh berries and raspberry syrup
   (see basics), to serve

Line a terrine or loaf pan with parchment paper and set aside. Put the sugar and a scant 2/3 cup water in a saucepan and bring to a boil, stirring until the sugar dissolves. Boil for 3 minutes. Remove from the heat and add the chocolate, stirring until the chocolate melts and the syrup is smooth.

Whisk the egg yolks in a bowl until pale. Slowly pour in the sugar syrup and continue to whisk until the mixture cools. Fold in the whipped cream, Frangelico, and almonds, and pour the mixture into the prepared pan. Cover and freeze overnight.

To serve, turn the parfait out from the pan and cut into six thick slices with a warm knife. Serve with fresh berries and raspberry syrup.

baked figs with pistachios

4 large figs
1¹/₂ tablespoons soft brown sugar
1 orange, zested and juiced
1¹/₂ tablespoons unsalted butter
¹/₃ cup pistachio nuts
¹/₂ teaspoon ground cinnamon
1 tablespoon honey
1 cup mascarpone cheese

Preheat the oven to 350°F. Slice the figs into quarters lengthwise from the top downward, being careful not to slice all the way through. Place them in a baking dish and put a heaping teaspoon of sugar and some orange zest into the center of each fig. Divide the butter between the figs and dot it on top of the sugar. Add the pistachios and orange juice to the dish and sprinkle with a little cinnamon. Bake the figs for 10 minutes.

Meanwhile, blend the honey into the mascarpone until smooth.

To serve, carefully remove the figs from the dish and put a spoonful of honeyed mascarpone in the middle of each. Spoon the juice and pistachios over the top and serve while still warm.

quince and rosewater tarts

makes 12

1/3 cup quince paste

4 tablespoons orange juice

1/2 cup mascarpone cheese

1/2 teaspoon rosewater

2 teaspoons confectioners' sugar

1 tablespoon ground almonds,
lightly toasted

12 prebaked sweet tartlet shells
(see basics)

Melt the quince paste with the orange juice in a bowl over a saucepan of simmering water. Stir well to combine, then remove and allow to cool.

Blend together the mascarpone, rosewater, confectioners' sugar, and ground almonds. Spoon the mixture into the tartlet shells and top with the cooled quince paste.

marinated raspberries with coconut ice

serves 4

3 tablespoons orange juice
1 tablespoon Grand Marnier (optional)
4 cups raspberries
3 tablespoons milk
1/2 cup sugar
1/2 cup confectioners' sugar
1/2 cup dried coconut
2 teaspoons butter
1/2 teaspoon orange-flower water
2 drops pink food coloring

Combine the orange juice and Grand Marnier in a small bowl. Very gently stir in the raspberries and leave for 30 minutes to marinate.

Bring the milk and both sugars to a boil and boil gently for 3 minutes. Add the coconut and butter and boil for 1 minute, then add the orange-flower water and pink food coloring. Remove from the heat and stir until the mixture resembles bread crumbs. Store in an airtight container until ready to use.

To serve, pile the raspberries into glasses or bowls and sprinkle with the coconut ice.

winter fruit crumble serves 6

7 stems rhubarb (about 10½ ounces), roughly chopped
1 orange, juiced
6 dried figs, finely sliced
2 green apples, peeled, cored, and roughly chopped
¼ cup superfine sugar
½ cup all-purpose flour
½ cup soft brown sugar
½ cup ground almonds
¼ cup unsalted butter
light whipping cream, to serve

Preheat the oven to 350°F. Toss the rhubarb with the orange juice, figs, apples, and superfine sugar. Tip the mixture into an ovenproof dish.

Put the flour, brown sugar, and ground almonds in a bowl, then add the butter and rub it into the dry ingredients until the mixture begins to resemble bread crumbs. Crumble the mixture over the fruit and bake for 45 minutes. Serve hot with cream.

honey-spiced figs   serves 4

8 figs
1 orange, juicee and zested
12 small mint leaves, torn
1 tablespoon honey
3/4 cup heavy cream
1/2 teaspoon superfine sugar
1 tablespoon ground walnuts

Slice the figs, then overlap them on a serving plate. Pour the orange juice over the top, then scatter with the orange zest and mint leaves. Drizzle with the honey and set aside.

Put the cream, sugar, and walnuts into a small bowl and stir to combine. Serve the cream with the figs.

pears baked in marsala

serves 6

6 ripe pears
3 1/2 tablespoons butter, softened
1/2 heaping cup soft brown sugar
1 lemon, zested and juiced
scant 2/3 cup Marsala
2 cinnamon sticks, roughly broken
heavy cream, to serve

Preheat the oven to 350°F. Using a small knife, remove the core from each of the pears. Cut a thin slice off of the base of each pear to allow them to sit easily. Spread the butter over the skins of the pears and stand them in a baking dish.

In a small bowl combine the sugar, lemon juice, and Marsala. Pour the mixture around the pears, then add the cinnamon sticks and lemon zest.

Cover the pears with foil and bake for 30 minutes, then lower the heat to 300°F and bake for an additional 30 minutes. Serve with heavy cream and spoonfuls of the baking juices.

pine-nut meringues with marinated raspberries serves 6

3 egg whites
1 cup superfine sugar
2/3 cup pine nuts
5 cups raspberries
1 teaspoon confectioners' sugar
1 tablespoon Grand Marnier
1 1/4 cups heavy cream

Preheat the oven to 275°F. Line a large baking sheet with parchment paper.

Beat the egg whites to form stiff peaks, then gradually whisk in the sugar a spoonful at a time. Continue to whisk until stiff and glossy.

Fold the pine nuts into the meringue. Spoon the mixture onto the prepared baking sheet, forming six mounds of meringue. Bake for 1 hour, then turn off the oven and allow the meringues to cool in the oven.

Put the raspberries in a bowl and sprinkle with the confectioners' sugar and Grand Marnier. Allow to sit for 5 minutes, then lightly toss so that the liquid coats all the raspberries.

Serve the meringues with a spoonful of berries and a dollop of heavy cream.

middle eastern summer fruit compote with honeyed yogurt

serves 4

1 cinnamon stick

2 star anise

1/2 cup sugar

2 peaches, pitted and cut into quarters

2 nectarines, pitted and cut into quarters

2 apricots, pitted and cut into quarters

2 plums, pitted and cut into quarters

1 1/2 cups raspberries

1 teaspoon rosewater

plain yogurt and honey, to serve

sugared rose petals, to garnish

Put the cinnamon stick, star anise, sugar, and 2 cups of water into a saucepan and bring to a boil. Stir to ensure that the sugar has dissolved then add all the fruit. Bring to a boil, then remove the fruit with a slotted spoon and place in a serving bowl. Reduce the heat and allow the syrup to simmer for an additional few minutes, then add the rosewater. Spoon the syrup over the fruit and chill until ready to serve.

Serve with yogurt drizzled with honey, garnished with sugared rose petals.

brandied oranges with mascarpone

serves 6

1 cup sugar
3 cardamom pods
2 star anise
1 cinnamon stick
6 oranges
2 tablespoons brandy
1 cup mascarpone cheese

Put the sugar, cardamom pods, star anise, and cinnamon stick in a heavy-based saucepan with 2/3 cup water. Heat over medium heat, stirring occasionally, until the sugar dissolves. Boil without stirring until the syrup begins to color, and continue to cook until the syrup turns a golden caramel. Remove the pan from the heat and carefully add 1/2 cup of warm water.

Peel the oranges, removing the pith, then slice crossways into thick slices. Reassemble the oranges and place in a deep ceramic or glass dish. Cover with the spiced syrup and brandy. Cover and chill until ready to serve.

Serve the oranges with a drizzle of sauce and a spoonful of mascarpone.

fig and honey smoothie berry smoothie rhubarb
smoothie chilled knight pimm's with ginger syrup
berry ice greyhound negroni smooth sambucca classic
rusty nail orange and rosewater ice cubes manhattan
long island iced tea peach tree hot toddy mai tai
mandarin ice with pomegranate hangover cure fig and
honey smoothie berry smoothie rhubarb smoothie
chilled knight pimm's with ginger syrup berry ice

05 drinks

greyhound negroni smooth sambucca classic rusty nail
orange juice with rosewater ice cubes manhattan long
island iced tea peach tree hot toddy mai tai
mandarin ice with pomegranate hangover cure fig
and honey smoothie berry smoothie rhubarb smoothie

fig and honey smoothie

serves 2

2 ripe black figs, roughly chopped
1 tablespoon honey
3/4 cup plain yogurt
8 ice cubes
3 tablespoons finely chopped walnuts

Combine the figs, honey, yogurt, and ice cubes in a blender and process until smooth. Pour into two glasses and lightly stir the walnuts through.

berry smoothie

1/2 cup strawberries
1/2 cup blackberries
1/2 cup raspberries
1/4 cup sugar syrup
1/4 cup plain yogurt
6 ice cubes

Combine all the ingredients in a blender and process until smooth. Pour into two chilled glasses and serve immediately.

rhubarb smoothie

serves 4

stewed rhubarb

7 stems rhubarb (about 10¹/₂ ounces)
¹/₄ cup superfine sugar

1¹/₂ cups plain yogurt
¹/₂ teaspoon ground cinnamon
16 ice cubes

Trim the rhubarb stems and cut each stem into four pieces. Put the rhubarb, sugar, and ¹/₄ cup water in a stainless steel saucepan over medium heat. Cover and simmer for 10 minutes. Remove from the heat and allow to cool.

In a blender, combine 1 cup of the cooled stewed rhubarb with the yogurt, cinnamon, and ice cubes. Blend until smooth. Pour the mixture into four chilled glasses and serve.

chilled knight

2 cups vermouth rosso
1/2 ounce Fernet Branca
1/2 cup seedless raisins
zest of 2 oranges
5 cardamom pods, crushed
6 cloves
1 tablespoon grated fresh ginger
2 cinnamon sticks
1 1/3 cups sugar
6 cups red wine, chilled
scant 1/2 cup dark rum
2 cups blanched almonds, toasted

Put the vermouth, Fernet Branca, raisins, orange zest, cardamom, cloves, ginger, cinnamon sticks, and sugar in a saucepan and bring to a boil over medium heat. Reduce the heat to low and simmer for 10 minutes. Remove and allow to cool.

Add the chilled wine, rum, and toasted almonds, and pour into a punch bowl or large pitcher.

Note—Chilled knight may be served cold as a spicy late-night summer's drink, or warmed as a mulled wine on a winter's night.

pimm's with ginger syrup

serves 1

ginger syrup
1/2 cup grated ginger
1 cup sugar

1/2 cup fresh pineapple juice
2 ounces Pimm's
4–5 ice cubes
1/4 cup soda water
lime slices and pineapple pieces,
  to garnish

To make the ginger syrup, place the ginger, sugar, and 1/2 cup water in a small saucepan and bring to a boil. Reduce the heat and simmer for 5 minutes. Strain into a container, allow to cool, then store in the refrigerator until ready to use.

Put the pineapple juice, Pimm's, and 1 1/2 tablespoons ginger syrup into a tall glass with ice. Top with soda water and garnish with lime and pineapple.

berry ice

sugar syrup
1 cup sugar
1 cup water

6 strawberries
1/2 cup frozen blackberries
2 ounces vodka
10 ice cubes

To make the sugar syrup, place the sugar and water in a small saucepan and bring to a boil, stirring until the sugar dissolves. Allow to cool, then store in a bottle in the refrigerator until ready to use.

Put the remaining ingredients in a blender with 1/4 cup of the sugar syrup and process to form an icy slush. Pour into two chilled cocktail glasses. Serve immediately.

greyhound

2 ounces vodka
scant 1/2 cup freshly squeezed
  grapefruit juice
dash of Cointreau or triple sec
ice, to serve

Put the vodka, grapefruit juice, and a dash of Cointreau or triple sec in a tall glass. Stir, then top with ice.

This drink is also suitable to serve in a large pitcher—simply increase the quantity accordingly.

negroni

ice, to serve
1 ounce Campari
1 ounce sweet vermouth
1 ounce gin
orange peel, to garnish

Fill two chilled glasses with ice and add the Campari, vermouth, and gin to each. Stir lightly to "marble" the three alcohols, and garnish with slices of orange peel.

smooth sambucca   serves 1

1 ounce crème de cacao
1 ounce Sambucca

Pour the crème de cacao into a shot glass. Add the Sambucca, pouring it over the back of a spoon so that the liqueurs form two distinct layers.

classic rusty nail   serves 1

1 ounce whiskey
1 ounce Drambuie
3 ice cubes

Put the whiskey, Drambuie, and ice cubes into a chilled glass. Stir well to combine. This is the perfect drink for a late winter's night and can be served with or without ice.

orange juice with rosewater ice cubes

serves 6

4 red organic roses, petals removed
1 cup sugar
1 tablespoon rosewater
freshly squeezed orange juice, to serve

Place the rose petals, sugar, and 1¼ cups water in a large saucepan and bring to a boil. Reduce the heat and simmer for 8 minutes, or until you have a light syrup. Remove any film as it forms. Allow to cool, then stir in the rosewater and 1 cup water. Pour into ice cube trays and freeze.

In six chilled glasses, serve the ice cubes with orange juice.

manhattan

ice, for chilling
2 ounces blended whiskey
1 ounce sweet vermouth
dash of Angostura bitters
lemon peel, for garnish

Fill a glass with ice, then add the whiskey, vermouth, and bitters. Stir until the alcohol has chilled, then strain into a chilled cocktail glass. Serve with a twist of lemon peel.

long island iced tea

serves 2

1 ounce vodka
1 ounce gin
1 ounce white rum
1 ounce white tequila
1 ounce triple sec
2 tablespoons lemon juice
8 ice cubes
cola, to serve
lemon wedges, to garnish

Put the vodka, gin, rum, tequila, triple sec, and lemon juice in a cocktail shaker with the ice and shake well. Pour into two chilled glasses with ice, and add some cola. Garnish with the lemon wedges.

peach tree   serves 1

ice cubes, to serve
1/4 cup peach syrup
2 ounces dark Jamaican rum
lime wedge, to garnish

Fill a small tumbler with ice and pour in the peach syrup and rum. Stir well and garnish with a wedge of lime. The syrup from poached summer fruit makes an ideal base for this drink.

hot toddy

serves 1

1/2 teaspoon soft brown sugar
1 strip lemon peel
1 clove
1 cinnamon stick
2 ounces whiskey

Put all the ingredients in a heatproof glass and top with boiling water.

mai tai

ice, to fill cocktail shaker, plus extra to
  serve
1 tablespoon lime juice
1 ounce Grand Marnier
dash of Angostura bitters
2 ounces dark Jamaican rum
1 teaspoon grenadine syrup
1/3 cup pineapple juice
2 drops almond extract
pineapple pieces and mint, to garnish

Fill a cocktail shaker with ice. Add all the liquid ingredients and shake well. Pour into a chilled glass over some extra ice and garnish with pineapple pieces and mint.

mandarin ice
with pomegranate

3/4 **cup freshly squeezed mandarin juice**
2 tablespoons sugar syrup
crushed ice, to serve
1/2 **pomegranate, juiced and strained**

Combine the mandarin juice and sugar syrup and pour into two glasses filled with crushed ice. Top each glass with pomegranate juice.

hangover cure

serves 1

2 ounces Fernet Branca
1 ounce vermouth rosso
1/2 ounce crème de menthe
ice, to serve

Pour the three liqueurs into a tumbler over ice, mix well, and serve.

chicken stock veal stock vegetable stock dashi stock lamb marinade chicken marinade buttered couscous crepe batter roasted tomato pasta sauce harissa vinaigrette mashed potatoes aioli tahini sauce croutons tamarind water lime sorbet chocolate tart shell short-crust tart shell short-crust tartlet shells cardamom almond bread orange mascarpone vanilla ice cream chocolate ice cream

06 basics

gingerbread raspberry syrup chicken stock veal stock vegetable stock dashi stock lamb marinade chicken marinade buttered couscous crepe mixture roasted tomato pasta sauce harissa vinaigrette mashed potatoes aioli tahini sauce croutons

chicken stock

1 whole fresh chicken
1 onion, sliced
2 celery stalks, sliced
1 leek, roughly chopped
1 bay leaf
a few sprigs Italian parsley
6 peppercorns

Fill a large heavy-based saucepan with 12 cups cold water. Cut the chicken into several large pieces and put them into the saucepan.

Bring just to a boil, then reduce the heat to a simmer. Skim any fat from the surface, then add the onion, celery stalks, leek, bay leaf, parsley sprigs, and peppercorns. Maintain the heat at a low simmer for 2 hours.

Strain the stock into a bowl and allow to cool. Using a large spoon, remove any fat that has risen to the surface.

For a more concentrated flavor, return the stock to a saucepan and simmer over low heat. If you are not using the stock immediately, cover and refrigerate or freeze it.

veal stock

2¼ pounds veal bones
2 tablespoons olive oil
2 chopped onions
3 garlic cloves
2 leeks, roughly chopped
2 celery stalks, sliced
2 large tomatoes, roughly chopped
1 bay leaf
6 black peppercorns

Preheat the oven to 400°F. Put the veal bones and olive oil into a large roasting pan, rub the oil over the bones, and bake for 30 minutes. Add the onions, garlic, leeks, celery, and tomatoes to the pan. Continue baking for about 1 hour, or until the bones are well browned.

Transfer the roasted bones and vegetables to a large heavy-based saucepan and cover with plenty of cold water. Bring to a boil over medium heat, then reduce the heat to a simmer. Skim any fat from the surface, then add the bay leaf and peppercorns. Cook at a low simmer for 4 hours. Strain the stock into a bowl and allow to cool.

With a large spoon, remove any fat on the surface. Return the stock to a saucepan. Simmer over low heat to reduce and concentrate the flavor.

vegetable stock makes about 8 cups

2 tablespoons unsalted butter
2 garlic cloves, crushed
2 onions, roughly chopped
4 leeks, coarsely chopped
3 carrots, coarsely chopped
3 celery stalks, thickly sliced
1 fennel bulb, coarsely chopped
1 handful Italian parsley
2 sprigs thyme
2 black peppercorns

Put the butter, garlic, and onions into a large, heavy-based saucepan. Over medium heat, stir until the onion is soft and transparent. Add the leeks, carrots, celery, fennel, parsley, thyme, and peppercorns. Add 16 cups of water and bring to a boil. Reduce the heat and simmer for 2 hours. Allow to cool.

Strain into another saucepan, using the back of a large spoon to press all the liquid from the vegetables. Bring the stock to a boil, then reduce the heat to a rolling boil until the stock reduces by half.

dashi stock

makes about 8 cups

12 pieces dried kombu
1 tablespoon bonito flakes

Put 8 cups cold water and the kombu in a saucepan and slowly bring to a boil over medium heat. Regulate the heat so that the water takes about 10 minutes to come to a boil. As it nears the boiling point, test the thickest part of the kombu: if it is soft and your thumbnail easily cuts into the surface, remove the kombu.

Bring the water back to a boil, then add half a glass of cold water and pour in the bonito flakes. As soon as the stock returns to a boil, remove it from the heat and skim the surface. When the bonito flakes have sunk to the bottom of the pan, strain the stock through a square of cheesecloth or a very fine sieve. The finished stock should be clear and free of bonito flakes.

Note–As an alternative to dashi stock, instant dashi is available in most large supermarkets, health food stores, or specialty Asian shops.

lamb marinade

1/2 **cup white wine**
4 tablespoons olive oil
juice of 1 lemon
1 tablespoon fresh oregano
1 garlic clove, finely chopped

Put all the ingredients in a bowl. Add lamb chops, loin chops, or a boned leg of lamb to the marinade. Toss to thoroughly coat the lamb, and marinate in the refrigerator for 2–3 hours.

Cook the lamb until it is still a little pink in the center. Season with sea salt and freshly ground black pepper. Allow to rest for 5 minutes before serving.

chicken marinade makes 1/2 cup

3 tablespoons lemon juice
3 tablespoons olive oil
1 tablespoon Dijon mustard
1 teaspoon finely chopped garlic
1 teaspoon thyme
1/2 teaspoon ground white pepper

Put all the ingredients in a large bowl. Add chicken pieces to the marinade and toss to coat, then marinate in the refrigerator for 2–3 hours.

Remove the chicken from the marinade and barbecue or roast until cooked. Season with sea salt and serve.

buttered couscous serves 4

1 cup instant couscous
3 tablespoons butter, chopped
sea salt and freshly ground black
  pepper, to serve

Bring 1 cup water to a boil in a saucepan and add the couscous. Take the pan off the heat, add the butter in small pieces, and leave to stand for 10 minutes.

Fluff up the couscous with a fork and season well with salt and freshly ground black pepper.

crepe batter

1 cup all-purpose flour
4 eggs
1 teaspoon baking powder
3$1/2$ tablespoons butter, melted
pinch salt
1$1/4$ cups milk

Whisk together the flour, eggs, baking powder, butter, and salt. Slowly add the milk and whisk until smooth. Allow the batter to sit for a few hours or preferably overnight.

roasted tomato pasta sauce

serves 4

6 plum tomatoes
10 basil leaves
1 garlic clove
1 teaspoon sugar
2 tablespoons extra-virgin olive oil
1 teaspoon balsamic vinegar

Preheat the oven to 400°F. Put the tomatoes on a baking sheet and roast until the skins begin to blacken all over.

Put the whole tomatoes, including the charred skin and any juices, into a food processor or blender with the remaining ingredients. Blend to form a thick sauce, thinning with a little warm water if necessary.

Toss the sauce through warm pasta and serve with grated Parmesan cheese and basil leaves.

harissa

2 red bell peppers
3 red chilies, seeded
2 garlic cloves
1 tablespoon cumin seeds, roasted
  and ground
1 tablespoon coriander seeds, roasted
  and ground
1 large handful cilantro leaves
1 tablespoon pomegranate molasses
1 teaspoon sea salt
2¹/₂ tablespoons olive oil

Preheat the oven to 415°F. Put the bell peppers on a baking sheet and roast until the skins have blistered and blackened. Remove and set aside to cool.

Remove the skin and seeds from the bell peppers and put the flesh in a food processor with the chilies, garlic, ground spices, cilantro, pomegranate molasses, and sea salt. Blend to a puree, then add the olive oil and process again.

vinaigrette

2 tablespoons vinegar
$1/2$ cup olive oil
1 teaspoon Dijon mustard

Whisk all the ingredients together and season to taste. You may want to add other herbs, such as fresh thyme, basil, or rosemary. Lemon juice can replace the vinegar.

mashed potatoes

4 large floury potatoes, peeled
2 tablespoons milk
3 tablespoons butter
sea salt and freshly ground black
  pepper, to season

Cut the potatoes into pieces. Cook in a saucepan of simmering water for 15 minutes or until soft. Drain well, then return the potatoes to the saucepan with the milk and butter. Mash until smooth. Season with salt and freshly ground black pepper.

aioli

2 egg yolks
2 large garlic cloves, crushed
sea salt and white pepper, to season
scant 1¹/₄ cups olive oil
1 lemon, juiced
¹/₄ teaspoon ground white pepper

Whisk together the egg yolks and garlic with a little sea salt. Begin to add the olive oil in a thin stream, whisking continuously. Add a little of the lemon juice, then continue whisking in the remaining oil. Fold in the remaining lemon juice and season with the white pepper and a little sea salt.

tahini sauce

1/2 cup tahini
1 lemon, juiced
2 tablespoons plain yogurt
1 teaspoon ground cumin

Put all the ingredients into a bowl and add 3 tablespoons water. Stir until well combined. Serve as a dressing for fish, chicken, or with spiced salads.

croutons

6 thick slices white bread
1/2 cup oil
sea salt and freshly ground black
  pepper, to season

Remove the crusts from the bread and cut the bread into small cubes.

Heat the oil in a frying pan, and when the surface of the oil starts to shimmer, add the bread cubes and reduce the heat. Toss the bread in the oil until the croutons are golden brown. Remove the croutons with a slotted spoon and drain on paper towels. Season with sea salt and freshly ground black pepper.

tamarind water

makes 2 cups

1/3 cup tamarind pulp

Put the tamarind pulp in a bowl and cover with 2 cups boiling water. Allow to steep for 1 hour, stirring occasionally to break up the fibers, then strain.

lime sorbet

serves 4

1 cup sugar
4–5 limes, zested and juiced

Dissolve the sugar in 4 cups water in a saucepan over low heat. Boil for 2–3 minutes, then remove from the heat. Allow to cool.

Add the lime juice to the sugar syrup with the zest of 1 lime. Taste, then stir in a little more lime zest if necessary. Allow to cool.

Put the mixture in an ice cream machine and churn according to the manufacturer's instructions.

chocolate tart shell

makes one 10-inch tart shell

2/3 cup unsalted butter

1½ cups all-purpose flour

2 tablespoons unsweetened cocoa powder

Put all the ingredients in a food processor and whiz to form a paste. If the pastry doesn't come together into a ball, add a dash of chilled water. Cover the pastry in plastic wrap and refrigerate for 30 minutes.

Roll the pastry out as thinly as possible—the easiest way to do this is between two layers of plastic wrap. Line a 10-inch tart pan with the pastry. Chill until ready to use.

Preheat the oven to 350°F. Cover the pastry with a layer of parchment paper weighted down with baking weights or uncooked rice. Bake for 15 minutes.

Remove the paper and weights and bake for an additional 5 minutes, or until the base of the pastry is cooked through and looks dry.

short-crust tart shell

1 2/3 cups all-purpose flour
heaping 1/3 cup unsalted butter
1 tablespoon superfine sugar
pinch salt

Put the flour, butter, sugar, and salt into a food processor and process for 1 minute. Add 2 tablespoons chilled water and pulse until the mixture comes together. Wrap the dough in plastic wrap and chill for 30 minutes.

Roll the pastry out as thinly as possible—the easiest way to do this is between two layers of plastic wrap. Line a greased 10-inch tart pan with the pastry and chill for 30 minutes.

Preheat the oven to 350°F. Prick the base of the pastry with a fork, line it with crumpled parchment paper, and fill with baking weights or uncooked rice. Bake for 10–15 minutes, or until the pastry looks cooked and dry. Remove and allow to cool.

Note—Unbaked tart shells that are not used immediately can be stored in the freezer for several weeks. Put the tart shell in a preheated oven directly from the freezer (thawing the pastry shell first is not necessary).

short-crust tartlet shells

makes 36 tartlet shells

1²/₃ cups all-purpose flour
heaping ¹/₃ cup unsalted butter
pinch salt

Put the flour, butter, and salt into a food processor and process for 1 minute. Add 2 tablespoons iced water and pulse until the mixture comes together. Wrap in plastic wrap and chill for 30 minutes.

Roll the pastry out and cut into rounds. Put into greased muffin or tartlet pans and chill for an additional 30 minutes.

Preheat the oven to 350°F. Prick the pastry bases with a fork and fill with baking weights or uncooked rice. Bake for 7–10 minutes, then remove and allow to cool.

Note—To make a sweet pastry, add 1 tablespoon superfine sugar or 1 teaspoon vanilla extract to the flour and butter mixture. Unbaked tartlet shells that are not used immediately can be stored in the freezer for several weeks. Place in a preheated oven directly from the freezer (thawing them first is not necessary).

cardamom almond bread

serves 4

3 egg whites
1/3 cup superfine sugar
2/3 cup all-purpose flour
2 oranges, zested
1/2 cup blanched almonds
1/4 teaspoon ground cardamom

Preheat the oven to 350°F. Grease a 3 x 9-inch loaf pan and line it with parchment paper.

Whisk the egg whites until they are stiff, then slowly whisk in the sugar. When the sugar has been fully incorporated and the egg whites are glossy, fold in the flour, orange zest, almonds, and cardamom. Spoon the mixture into the prepared pan and bake for 40 minutes.

Cool the almond bread on a wire rack. When it is cold, cut it into thin slices with a serrated knife and spread the slices out on a baking sheet. Bake at 275°F for 15 minutes, or until crisp.

Allow the bread to cool on a wire rack before storing in an airtight container.

orange mascarpone

2 eggs, separated
2 tablespoons sugar
1 tablespoon grated orange zest
1 tablespoon Grand Marnier
1 heaping cup mascarpone cheese

Beat the egg whites until stiff, then set aside. Beat the egg yolks with the sugar and orange zest until light and creamy. Gently whisk in the Grand Marnier and mascarpone, then fold the egg whites through. Chill for 1 hour.

vanilla ice cream

8 egg yolks
scant 1/2 cup superfine sugar
1 1/2 cups milk
1 1/2 cups light whipping cream
1 vanilla bean, split

Whisk together the egg yolks and sugar until thick and creamy. Put the milk and cream in a saucepan with the split vanilla bean. Bring just to a boil, then pour the hot milk mixture into the sugar and egg mixture while still whisking.

Pour the custard back into the saucepan and continue to stir over a low heat until the custard is thick enough to coat the back of a wooden spoon. Remove the vanilla bean and scrape the seeds into the mixture.

Put the cooled mixture into an ice-cream maker and churn according to the manufacturer's instructions.

Alternatively, put it in a freezer-proof container and freeze. Take the ice-cream mixture out of the freezer every couple of hours and beat it. This will break up any ice crystals as they form and make the ice cream creamier.

chocolate ice cream

serves 4

1 1/2 cups milk
1 cup light whipping cream
2/3 cup roughly chopped dark
  chocolate
4 egg yolks
1/3 cup caster (superfine) sugar
2 tablespoons unsweetened cocoa
  powder

Put the milk, cream, and chocolate in a heavy-based saucepan over medium heat. Bring the milk and cream just to simmering point, stirring to help the chocolate melt. Remove the saucepan from the heat. Put the egg yolks and caster sugar in a mixing bowl and whisk until light and foamy. Add the cocoa powder and whisk again. Whisk in a little of the warm chocolate mixture. Add the remaining liquid and whisk to combine. Return the mixture to a clean saucepan. Cook over medium heat, stirring with a wooden spoon, until the mixture thickens and coats the back of the spoon. Strain into a bowl and allow to cool. Churn in an ice-cream machine according to the manufacturer's instructions.

gingerbread

1/2 cup butter
1/2 cup sugar
1/4 cup molasses
1 egg
1 1/2 cups all-purpose flour
1 teaspoon baking powder
2 teaspoons ground ginger
1/2 teaspoon ground cinnamon
2 tablespoons preserved ginger in
  syrup, grated
3 tablespoons brandy

Preheat the oven to 325°F. Line a 9 x 5 x 3-inch loaf pan with waxed paper. Beat together the sugar and butter until light and fluffy. Beat in the molasses and egg. Work in the dry ingredients, then fold in the preserved ginger and brandy. Pour into the prepared pan and bake for 1 hour 45 minutes, or until a skewer inserted into the center of the cake comes out clean. Serve in thick slices.

raspberry syrup makes about 1/2 cup

1/2 cup sugar
1 cup raspberries

Put the sugar and raspberries into a saucepan with 1/2 cup water and bring to a boil.

Stir until the sugar has dissolved, then reduce the heat to low. Allow to simmer for 5 minutes, remove from the heat, and allow to cool.

Blend to a puree in a food processor or blender, then strain through a fine sieve into a jug.

glossary

balsamic vinegar

Balsamic vinegar is a dark, fragrant, sweetish aged vinegar made from grape juice. Bottles of the real thing have "Aceto Balsamico, Tradizionale de Modena" written on the label.

basil

The most commonly used basil is the sweet or Genoa variety that is much favored in Italian cooking. Thai or holy basil is used in Thai and Southeast Asian dishes.

black sesame seeds

Mainly used in Asian cooking, black sesame seeds add color, crunch, and a distinct nuttiness to whatever dish they garnish.

brown miso

Brown miso (hatcho miso) is a fermented paste of soy beans, salt, and either rice or barley. It is available from Asian stores and health food shops.

bulgur wheat

Bulgur is the key ingredient in tabouleh. Steamed and baked to minimize cooking time, you can buy these wheat kernels either whole or cracked into fine, medium, or coarse grains.

Cajun spice mix

A spice blend available in ready-mixed packets from most supermarkets. The predominant flavors are cumin, cayenne pepper, chili, mustard, and mixed herbs.

capers

Capers are green buds from a Mediterranean shrub preserved in brine or salt. Salted capers have a firmer texture and are often smaller than those preserved in brine. Rinse before using. Capers are available from good delicatessens.

cardamom

A dried seed pod native to India, cardamom is used whole or ground and can be found in the spice section of most supermarkets.

Chinese black beans

These salted black beans can be found either vacuum-packed or in cans in Asian food stores.

Chinese black vinegar

This rice vinegar is sharper than white rice varieties and is traditionally used in stir-fries, soups, and dipping sauces.

Chinese five-spice

This aromatic mix of ground spices is made from black pepper, star anise, fennel seeds, cassia, and cloves.

chipotle chilies

Chipotle chilies are available in cans from delicatessens preserved in a smoky rich sauce, or they can be bought as large smoked and dried chilies, which need to be reconstituted in warm water prior to use.

coconut cream

Slightly thicker than coconut milk, coconut cream is available in cans.

cream of tartar

This fine white powder is the acidic ingredient in baking powder and is often used to stablize egg whites.

crème de framboise

A raspberry liqueur.

crème fraîche

A naturally soured cream that is lighter than sour cream. It is available at gourmet food stores and some large supermarkets.

curry leaves

These are the smallish, green, aromatic leaves of a tree native to India and Sri Lanka. They are usually either fried and added to a dish or used as a garnish at the end.

daikon

Daikon, or mooli, is a large white radish. It can be grated or used in broths. It's available from large supermarkets or Asian grocery stores.

enoki mushrooms

These pale, delicate mushrooms have long, thin stalks and tiny caps. They are very fragile and need only a minimal cooking time.

feta cheese

Feta is a white cheese made from sheep or goat milk. It must be kept in the whey or in oil during storage, or it will deteriorate rapidly. Feta is available from delicatessens and most supermarkets.

fish sauce

This is a highly flavored, salty liquid made from fermented fish and widely used in South Asian cuisine to give a salty, savory flavor.

Frangelico

A hazelnut-flavored Italian liqueur sold in a brown bottle shaped like a monk's robe.

galangal

Galangal is quite perfumed and almost a little like camphor. Its root is quite fibrous and hard, making it difficult to chop. Galangal can be bought fresh or sliced and preserved in brine in bottles from Asian stores.

gelatin powder

Powdered gelatin may vary in strength so always check the manufacturer's instructions before using. It is available from supermarkets.

goat cheese

Also called chévre, this soft, fresh cheese made from goat milk has a mild, creamy flavor.

Gruyère cheese

A firm cow-milk cheese with a smooth texture

and natural rind. It has a nutty flavor and melts easily, making it perfect for tarts and gratins.

haloumi cheese
Haloumi is a semifirm sheep-milk cheese. It has a rubbery texture that becomes soft when the cheese is broiled or fried.

horseradish
Horseradish is the root of the mustard family—large and white, it has a knobbly brown skin. It is very pungent and has a spicy, hot flavor.

jaggery
Also called palm sugar, jaggery is obtained from the sap of various palm trees. If it is very hard, it will need to be grated.

jalapeño chilies
Small pickled jalapeño chilies are available in jars in the Mexican or gourmet section of speciality stores and large supermarkets.

Japanese eggplant
Much smaller and straighter in shape than the conventional eggplant, the Japanese variety also has softer and sweeter flesh.

Kaffir lime leaves
Also known as makrut, the glossy leaves of this Southeast Asian tree impart a wonderful citrusy aroma. Always try to use fresh leaves.

lavash bread
A Jewish-style bread that is sold fresh as thin, unleavened squares or dried in sheets similar to a crispbread.

Marsala
Perhaps Italy's most famous fortified wine, Marsala is available in sweet and dry varieties. Often used in desserts such as zabaglione, it is a superb match with eggs, cream, and almonds.

mascarpone cheese
This heavy, Italian-style set cream is used as a base in many sweet and savory dishes. It is made from cream rather than milk. It is sold in delicatessens and supermarkets.

mirin
Mirin is a rice wine used in Japanese cooking. It is available from Asian grocery stores and most large supermarkets.

miso paste
Miso paste is made from fermented soy beans and other flavorings — wheat, rice, or barley. It is used as a flavoring and a condiment.

mustard seeds
Mustard seeds have a sharp, hot flavor that is tempered by cooking. Both brown and yellow are available.

pancetta
Pancetta is salted pork belly. It is sold in good delicatessens and some supermarkets.

papaya

This large tropical fruit can be orange, red, or yellow. Sometimes called a pawpaw, they are really part of the custard apple family.

pepitas

These edible pumpkin seeds are popular in Mexican cooking. Pepitas are sold salted, roasted and raw, and with or without their white hull.

pickled ginger

Japanese pickled ginger is available from most large supermarkets. The thin slivers of young ginger root are pickled in sweet vinegar.

pomegranate molasses

This is a syrup made from the reduction of pomegranate juice. It is available from Middle Eastern speciality stores.

preserved lemon

These are whole lemons preserved in salt or brine for about 30 days, which turns their rind soft and pliable. Just the rind is used—the pulp should be scraped out and thrown away. Preserved lemon is an ingredient commonly found in Moroccan cooking.

prosciutto

Prosciutto is lightly salted, air-dried ham. It is most commonly bought in paper-thin slices and is available from large supermarkets.

pumpernickel

A dark, heavy-textured rye bread leavened with a sourdough culture, pumpernickel can be bought from delicatessens and supermarkets.

Puy lentils

Originally grown in the volcanic soils of the Puy region in France, these lentils are highly prized for their flavor and the fact that they hold their shape during cooking. Also called French green lentils.

quince paste

Quinces are large, aromatic fruits with a high pectin content. Quince paste can be purchased at most delicatessens.

rice paper wrappers

Rice paper wrappers are made of rice and water paste and are sold in thin, round, or square sheets, which soften when soaked in water. They are available from most large supermarkets or from speciality Asian stores.

rice wine vinegar

Made from fermented rice, this vinegar comes in clear, red, and black versions. If no color is specified in a recipe, use the clear vinegar.

saffron threads

These are the orange-red stigmas from one species of the crocus plant. Saffron should be bought in small quantities and used sparingly.

sambal oelek

A hot paste made from pounded chilies, salt, and vinegar, sambal oelek is available from Asian grocery stores and large supermarkets.

Shaoxing wine

Shaoxing wine is similar to a fine sherry and is made from glutinous rice. It is available from Asian grocery stores.

shiitake mushrooms

These Asian mushrooms have white gills and a brown cap. Meaty in texture, they keep their shape very well when cooked.

Szechuan pepper

These are from the dried red berries of the prickly ash tree, which is native to Szechuan in China. Their flavor is spicy-hot.

smoked paprika

Paprika is commonly sold as a dried, rich-red powder. It comes in many grades, from delicate, to sweet, and finally to hot.

sumac

Sumac is a peppery, sour spice made from dried and ground sumac berries. It is available at most large supermarkets.

tahini

This is a thick paste made from husked and ground white sesame seeds. Tahini is available from health food stores and supermarkets.

tamarind

Tamarind is the sour pulp of an Asian fruit. It is available compressed into cakes or refined as tamarind concentrate in jars.

tarama

The orange-colored salted and dried roe of the grey mullet, tarama is used in the preparation of authentic taramaslata.

tofu

This white curd is made from soy beans. Usually sold in blocks, there are several different types of tofu—soft (silken), firm, sheets, and deep-fried.

tortillas

This thin, round, unleavened bread is used in Mexican cooking as a wrap. Tortillas are available prepackaged in supermarkets.

turmeric

Turmeric is made from the root of a tropical plant related to ginger.

vanilla

The long, slim, black vanilla bean has a wonderful caramel aroma. Good-quality beans should be soft and not too dry.

white miso

White miso is the fermented paste of soy beans, salt, and either rice or barley. It is available from Asian grocery stores.

index

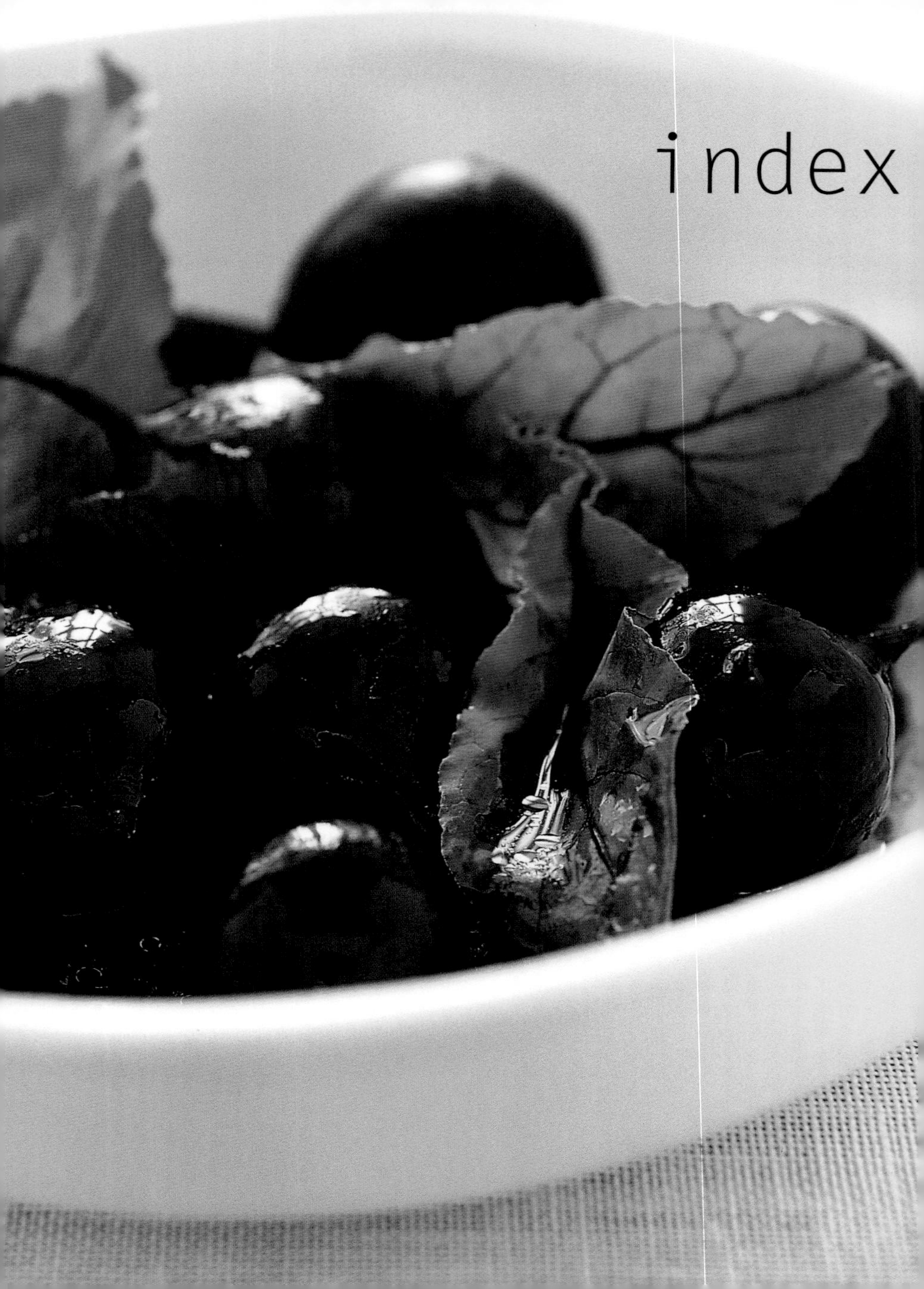